TAKING A STAND AGAINST RACISM AND RACIAL DISCRIMINATION

TAKING A STAND

AGAINST
RACISM AND
RACIAL
DISCRIMINATION

BY PATRICIA AND FREDRICK McKISSACK

Franklin Watts 1990
New York London Toronto Sydney

Photographs courtesy of: The Bettmann Archive: pp. 17, 20, 64, 80, 83; Gamma Liaison: p. 24 (John Chiasson); UPI/Bettmann Newsphotos: pp. 70, 73, 76, 81, 89, 93, 95, 100, 118, 139;

Photo Researchers: pp. 41 (Blair Seitz), 142 (Peter G. Aitken).
"Incident" (p. 39) by Countee Cullen reprinted by permission of GRM Associates, Inc., copyright 1925 by Harper & Brothers; copyright renewed 1953 by Ida M. Cullen.

Library of Congress Cataloging-in-Publication Data

McKissack, Pat, 1944–
Taking a stand against racism and racial discrimination / by Patricia and Fredrick McKissack.
p.   cm.
Includes bibliographical references (p.   )
Summary: Examines racism and racial discrimination in the United States, and the individuals and organizations who have acted against it.
ISBN 0-531-10924-0
1. Racism—United States—Juvenile literature.   2. Race discrimination—United States—Juvenile literature.   3. United States—Race relations—Juvenile literature.   [1. Racism.   2. Race discrimination.   3. Prejudices.   4. Race relations.]   I. McKissack, Fredrick.   II. Title.
E184.A1M3493   1990
305.8′00973—dc20   89-28627   CIP   AC

For our son,
Robert Lewis McKissack

CONTENTS

Although some people may discriminate against me, I shall never become bitter or lose faith. I am firm in my belief that American sportsmanship and the attitude of fair play will judge citizenship and patriotism on the basis of action and achievement, and not on the basis of physical characteristics.

Creed of the Japanese American
Citizens League, 1940

TAKING A STAND AGAINST RACISM
AND RACIAL DISCRIMINATION

ONE

WHY TAKE A STAND AGAINST RACISM AND RACIAL DISCRIMINATION?

Have you ever decided beforehand that you weren't going to have a good time at a party, and then had fun in spite of yourself? Did you ever refuse to sit beside a person at lunch because your other friends might not approve? Have you ever come to a conclusion without knowing all the facts? How long does it take you to taste a different food? Ever wonder why?

Anytime you've had one of these favorable or unfavorable feelings about a person or thing prior to, or not based on, actual experience, you have been guilty of prejudice.

PREJUDICE: THE ROOTS OF RACISM AND DISCRIMINATION

The word prejudice comes from the Latin noun *praejudicium*, which means "a judgment based on previous decisions formed before the facts were known."

Today, prejudice has a racial connotation, unfortunate because, as the examples above show, not all prejudice is racial. Racism is a specific kind of prejudice, based on "faulty reasoning and inflexible generalizations" directed toward a specific group. If a person allows his or her prejudiced beliefs to impede the progress of another, it is *discrimination*. Those who exclude all members of a race from certain types of employment, residential housing, political rights, educational opportunities, or social interaction are guilty of *racial discrimination*. At the core of most discriminatory acts is prejudice, and racism is usually the motivating factor.[1]

Many people, whether or not they admit it, have felt urges and emotions based on race prejudices. This is the dark side of our character, and people don't like to think of themselves in such an uncomplimentary way. Even the most radical groups defend their beliefs while vehemently denying they are bigoted.

RACISM HAS ANCIENT BEGINNINGS

For centuries periodic conflicts have taken place among the three principal races—Caucasian, Mongoloid, and Negroid—ranging from snobbish social exclusion to state-sponsored genocide. Racism, an unmerited fear or dislike of a people because of their ethnic heritage, is neither unique in the course of human relationships nor peculiar to any historical period, place, or people. Hatred and bigotry have ancient roots.

While sociologists and historians generally agree that at the core of most discriminatory acts is racial intolerance, discrimination is not confined to race alone. When color is not a factor, other rea-

14

sons such as language, religion, nationality, education, sex, or age become the basis of prejudice.

For example, the ancient Egyptians enslaved Hebrews because the pharaoh feared their growing numbers; the Greeks considered themselves superior to the Nordic peoples; the Romans referred to Germans as "blond barbarians" and forbade intermarriage; Japanese and Chinese armies clashed for thousands of years; and Islamic Africans sold other Africans, considered infidels, into slavery.[2] The most infamous chapter on ethnic hatred was the systematic murder of six million Jews in Nazi concentration camps during World War II.

HOW RACISM AND DISCRIMINATION DEVELOP

Sociologists, historians, anthropologists, and archeologists believe racial discrimination occurs more often and most severely when two groups with different skin colors and distinctive physical features come into contact with each other and the two compete for the same resources. What happens follows the same pattern worldwide, with predictable outcomes.

Groups A and B live in the same area, but they are from different racial groupings. Either by choice or by force, the groups do not interact. In time, Group A grows stronger than Group B. Group A enjoys all the advantages of political power and social acceptance. They also take a disproportionate amount of the resources, jobs, and goods—the wealth. In order to maintain their powerful position, Group A denies Group B the right of participation, and justifies the exclusion by stereotyping Group B as inferior. If the prejudiced attitudes are left unchallenged, they become accepted truths, becoming stronger as each generation passes them down to the next.

But history clearly shows that all attempts at racial dominance result in conflict and confrontation. On the other hand, a society free of disruptive racial strife can take advantage of all its citizens' potential and move toward maximum productivity.

AMERICAN RACISM

Economic greed has been cited as the primary source of American bigotry toward people of color. There is no denying fortunes were made in the slave trade.

Africans were brought to the colonies and forced to labor a lifetime for no wages. The master took all the profits, save the meager amount he used to provide food, clothing, and shelter for his slaves. Records show that in some cases horses and livestock fared better than did the slaves. Mexican, Native American, and Asian workers, though not formally enslaved, were also exploited for economic gain.

In order for this kind of human exploitation to continue in a nation founded on the principles of freedom and justice, some justification was needed. Racism provided a ready answer. Children were taught from infancy that people of color were dif-

*Plan for a
slave ship*

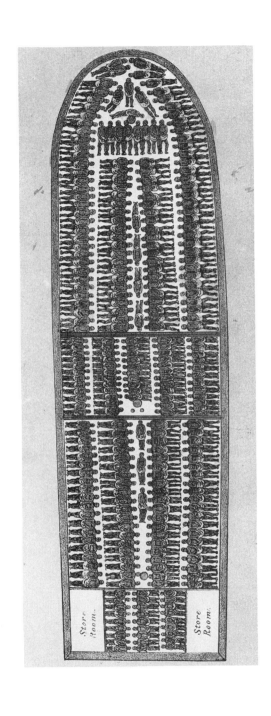

Store Room.

Store Room.

ferent and therefore unequal. To prove it, a systematic program of dehumanization was instituted.

By law, slaves were forbidden an education. They were cut off from their African language, religion, and history. All traces of the advanced West African cultures of Ghana, Mali, and Songhay were erased from European-American history. Africa was pictured as the "dark continent," its inhabitants mere savages in need of white salvation. Slave families were deliberately separated—husbands sold from wives, children sold from mothers—like cattle. Bible quotes, taken out of context, were used to support white dominance over all other races. Even the U.S. Constitution referred to a slave as "three-fifths" of a human being.[3]

Without the ability to read or write the first Africans in America had no defense against this denial of their humanity. The dehumanization of the African-American slave stands out as one of the most brutal and savage persecutions in history.

WHERE DID GOVERNMENT STAND?

President Abraham Lincoln signed the Emancipation Proclamation of 1863 freeing four million black men, women, and children living in Confederate states. The Proclamation did not take widespread effect until after the Civil War ended. But with no jobs, no education, and no resources, the former slaves' freedom was a mockery. Whites, who had been raised to believe they belonged to a superior race, refused to accept the freedmen as their equals. Although the physical chains of slavery were removed, the mental chains, forged by years of racism, kept all Americans in bondage for over one hundred years.

Resistance to racial equality was fiercest in the South, where white supremacy sentiment ran rampant. Extremist groups like the Ku Klux Klan used violence to terrorize former slaves and keep them "in their place." Beatings and lynchings, house and business burnings were common occurrences. The Klan's doctrine was that white Protestants were the rightful rulers of America. People of color, Catholics, and Jews were meant to be dominated by them. Anybody who did not go along with them was considered an enemy and they too were harassed.

Not all whites held bigoted and prejudiced attitudes. Many who did not were powerful men and women who used their influence to bring about changes. Some were ordinary people who would not take part in a system they believed was wrong. In spite of the stumbling blocks before them, men and women of color made significant contributions to the growth and development of America.

Still the centuries-old negative attitudes about blacks prevailed. The Thirteenth, Fourteenth and Fifteenth Amendments to the United States Constitution abolished slavery and granted slaves full citizenship and all men the right to vote. Yet ways were found to take those rights away. Between 1876 and 1900 state laws were passed prohibiting blacks from voting, holding public office, serving on juries, living in certain neighborhoods, or marrying a person of another race.

In *Plessy* v. *Ferguson,* the historic Supreme Court decision of 1896, segregation of the races was ruled constitutional if provisions were made for blacks that were equal to those for whites. This

The "separate but equal" clause of the
Supreme Court's 1896 Plessy v. Ferguson
decision led to "Jim Crow" laws mandating
racial segregation in many southern states.

"separate but equal" clause made it possible for states to segregate legally while the federal government looked the other way.[4]

As William Taylor of the Center for National Policy Review, a Washington, D.C., civil rights group, has said "Separation breeds fear and misunderstanding." The best way for racism to flourish is through ignorance and separation.

America had always been a racially divided nation, but the overruling of Reconstruction legislation made segregation legal once again by the turn of the century.

Within a year or two after the *Plessy* v. *Ferguson* decision, black people were forced to ride in the back of buses, drink from separate water fountains in public places, enter theaters from rear doors, attend schools that were anything but equal, and submit to all kinds of other indignities. They were paid less to do more work, hired last, and fired first. Substandard housing was very often all that was available and the rents were unreasonably high.

For the most part, blacks and whites lived apart, but more so in the South. Other minorities were subjected to this kind of legalized discrimination. For example, Native Americans were forced to live on reservations where life was harsh and the restrictions severe. Asians and Hispanics went to segregated schools and churches and lived in different neighborhoods. They also worked for lower wages. Even European immigrants who came to America seeking a better way of life found that acceptance was not automatic. They had to drop all cultural ties—language, dress, customs—and become "white Americans" before they could make advances. Those who held on to their customs and beliefs were social outcasts and shunned.

Without power, minorities were forced to the bottom of the economic, educational, and social ladder and kept there by unjust laws and violence. Unfortunately, children grew up believing *different* meant being inferior and living life as a second-class citizen. And by not enforcing the Constitution, the federal government seemed to give substance to that assumption.

In 1954, the Supreme Court's *Brown* v. *Board of Education of Topeka* struck down the "separate but equal" ruling of the 1896 court. This decision set the stage for the 1960s civil rights movement. The government took an active part in enforcing existing laws and statutes and in writing new laws.

By the end of the '60s, landmark civil rights legislation had been passed. Discrimination based on race, religion, or national origin was declared illegal. Jobs opened up. Schools integrated. Minority participation in government increased. The government had taken a stand against racial discrimination. Presidents Kennedy and Johnson strongly supported the passage of civil rights legislation. They set the tone for the rest of the country, and great strides in race relations were made, from small towns to large urban centers.

More opportunities were available to minorities in engineering, science, business, medicine, education, and other fields. When racism is not a factor, minorities have a high performance record. When the federal government took a stand and decided to assist in stopping racial discrimination, many people thought, mistakenly, that racism would be a dead issue by the twenty-first century. But developments in the 1980s showed that race prejudice is still very much alive.[5]

RESURGENCE OF RACISM

Discrimination is an *action*. It can be controlled. The federal government set up agencies and wrote tomes of guidelines to enforce civil rights laws. Still racism persists, because it is an *attitude* which cannot be so easily detected or legislated away.

So in spite of the substantial gains made in the 1960s, people found ways to get around the law. In the areas of housing, education, and employment, blacks and other minorities still lag behind whites. The results of a recent *Time* magazine poll showed that 92 percent of blacks and 87 percent of whites believed "racial prejudice is still common in America."

The mayor of Birmingham (called *Boomingham* during the 1960s because of the high number of racially motivated house and church bombings) said in the February 2, 1987 issue of *Time*, "In the past seven years racial progress has been at a standstill, and I'm inclined to say in a slight retreat."

According to FBI reports, Klan membership is increasing and minority beatings and murders have been traced to white supremacy groups. The all-white community of Howard Beach, New York, was the scene of a brutal beating of three blacks, one of whom was killed as he tried to escape across a highway and was hit by a passing car.

Forsyth County, Georgia, reminded the nation of its recent past when robed Ku Klux Klansmen

A racially motivated attack on three black men, one of whom was killed crossing a highway in an attempt to escape, in Howard Beach, New York, in 1986 prompted this protest march.

interrupted a peaceful protest march. At The Citadel, a military academy in Charleston, South Carolina, black cadets were subjected to racist hazing. Los Angeles Dodger vice-president Al Campanis and popular sportscaster Jimmy the Greek were forced to resign from their positions because of stereotypical racial remarks they made about black athletes.[5]

When minorities review their history in America, they are shocked and angered by the pattern of progress inevitably followed by white backlash and regression. Many minority youths lose their faith in the system and respond angrily or suspiciously toward even those who legitimately want to help. Today there is a great deal of irrational hostility directed toward whites by young blacks and Hispanics who are angry and frustrated.

TAKING A STAND

What disease has not been cured because a young doctor was denied equal opportunity? What houses have not been built because a contractor couldn't get a bank loan? What book has not been written? What child has not been taught? Those who would build fences and close doors only impede progress for us all. Rev. Jesse Jackson has said, "In order to keep a person in the gutter you have to be there yourself to make sure he stays."[6]

Sometimes people who are not racists will conform to popular opinion and adhere to prescribed social patterns because they want to be accepted; they don't want to lose their jobs or jeopardize their personal safety. Racism is secure when people choose to be silent, because silence seems to lend acceptance.

The battle against racism begins from within and moves out. Once an individual feels free enough to take a stand, then others will follow. Racism cannot thrive when a community says *we will not tolerate these attitudes and actions.*

Taking a stand against racism and racial discrimination, internally and externally, is a personal investment in your own mental growth and development and in the place where you live. When people live in harmony, celebrating their differences rather than using them to alienate and isolate, America becomes stronger and growth can take place without discriminatory violence and overt and covert acts of hate.

Where do you stand?

TWO

FORMS OF RACISM

When is the last time you questioned your beliefs and attitudes? Perhaps it is time.

Bigotry is like an insidious disease. Before a disease can be treated and cured it has to be diagnosed. So before you can take a stand against racism and race discrimination, you need to know what it is, how it develops, and how to recognize it in yourself and in others.

Begin by making a list of what you believe about people of other races. Include both negative and positive items. Then ask why you believe the things you do. If you don't have an answer leave it blank. Finally, list the evidence (proof, facts) you use to support each belief. Analyze your findings after reading this chapter, which provides an overview of the development of prejudice, discrimination, and the minority responses to it.

According to Alfred Fleishman, St. Louis newspaper columnist, "Racial prejudice is one of the scourges of our society. And when it grows and lurks, especially where it's not even noticed, the danger is even greater."

GENERALIZATIONS
AND MISCONCEPTIONS

Children are not born with prejudices of any kind. Prejudices begin with generalizations (vague and indefinite statements) and misconceptions (incorrect interpretations of information). Here are two examples of each.

After one date with a baseball player, a teenage girl generalizes that all athletes are dumb. The *one* baseball player is her only supportive evidence.

Although her reasoning is faulty, it is not inflexible, because when her brother and several good friends become athletes, she reevaluates her position. Her brother is smart; he is also an athlete. Some of her friends are good students and also good athletes. She notices in class that athletes vary in ability the same as other groups. Through observation and contact, she realizes that *all* athletes are not academically inferior. As she becomes better informed her conclusions become more accurate.

If the girl had not made the effort to correct her faulty thinking, the generalization could have become the basis of a prejudice, which is "faulty reasoning and *inflexible generalizations*."[10]

Similarly, at age seven a boy sees a spy film in which a Russian, disguised as an American citizen, steals important secret documents, causing widespread death and destruction. John concludes all Russians are dangerous spies.

He never shares his feelings with anyone, so left alone to draw his own conclusions, his misconception grows to the point that when Soviet immigrants move into the same apartment building where he lives, the boy becomes obsessed with fear. There are spies living in his building!

He can't understand his mother's suggestion to play with the "spy-children." And, when his father invites the family to dinner, the boy is rude and unkind. There is only one answer, he thinks. His parents have gone over to the other side. Feeling responsible for protecting his family and country, he calls the FBI and reports the situation.

When it is discovered, the boy's parents are shocked. They wonder where *their son* had gotten his ideas. Finally, he discusses his fears openly and his parents clear up the misconception.

What if the boy's fear about all Russians being spies had not been corrected? Clearly it might have been the foundation upon which a serious prejudice could have formed.[7]

BELIEFS AND ATTITUDES

From birth to about age twelve, children gather information about their world. They learn from many sources including their school, family, neighbors, friends, and the community at large. They also get information from books, movies, television, and other media. From this information they shape beliefs, attitudes, and opinions.[8]

A belief is a strong conviction, a trust or confidence placed in a person, idea, or thing. An opinion is a belief, according to *Webster's Ninth New Collegiate Dictionary*, that is "stronger than impression and less strong than positive knowledge." Attitudes are feelings and emotions held toward a person, idea, or thing. Attitude, opinions, and the way we treat people are based on our beliefs.

If beliefs are prejudiced, then attitude and behavior will correspond. Racism is a belief system founded on faulty reasoning, misconceptions, and generalizations.[8]

WHERE RACISM CAN LEAD

Racists have very specific beliefs about their own groups and others. Even the most well-meaning people sometimes fall prey to prejudice. Columnist Ellen Futterman of the St. Louis *Post-Dispatch* has written, "We are all guilty of race prejudice. We might go out of our way to avoid certain words and phrases in our everyday speech only to find ourselves laughing at a racial or ethnic joke later."[9] Futterman forces us to look inside and recognize a blemish in our character. But introspection is a necessary step in preparing to take a stand.

Stereotyping is an exaggerated belief associated with a group. For example, "all politicians are crooks." That is a greatly exaggerated, stereotyped generalization. Not *all* politicians are untrustworthy. But where did such a notion originate? As with any stereotype, there was an original model from which the generalization was made. No doubt there are some crooked politicians. But the watchword in recognizing a stereotype is *all*.

Stereotyping is perpetuated by name calling, racial slurs, and jokes. The excuse given most often is that "talk" is all "in fun," and no real harm is done to anyone. The idea that stereotyping is harmless is ludicrous. Social commentator Walter Lippmann warned over two generations ago that stereotypes create "indelible pictures in the head."[11] These fixed images shape and limit our attitudes about and behavior toward others.

Take for example the insensitive remark made by Calvin Griffith, owner of the Washington (D.C.) Senators. He moved the team to Minnesota when, in his own words, "I found out you only had 15,000 blacks here. Black people don't go to ball games, but they'll fill up a rasslin' ring and put up such a chant it'll scare you to death." Griffith's statement stereotyped black people and painted a very negative group image. When a person of Griffith's professional status makes a public comment containing such overt stereotyping, it only serves to legitimize racial myths.[12]

Racial stereotyping causes people to mistrust each other. Consider this hypothetical case: It is evening and a female employee is taking an elevator from the fifteenth floor to the ground level. While she is waiting, a black teenager joins her in the hallway. When the elevator doors open, the woman doesn't get on. The black youth takes offense at the implication of her actions, and shouts, "What's the matter? You think I'll mug you or something?"

The young man voices his suspicions that the woman's behavior is based on a racial stereotype— black teens are potential muggers. But that may or may not be the case. Perhaps this woman makes a point not to ride alone in an elevator with *any person*, male or female, because of the potential danger. But if she believed her situation was more threatening because the passenger was a black teen, then clearly the woman would have been guilty of stereotyping.

As the feelings of race prejudice become more intensified, the next stage is *avoidance*. Avoiders are those who react to their fears by choosing isolation from those who are different. Their world is divided into "them" or "those people" as opposed to "us." "If I stay away from them, then I will never have to deal with them," is a typical attitude. Avoiders may tolerate working or going to school with other races but social contact is out of the question. They will not read a book written by or about another race or live next door to a minority family. Avoiders feel secure within the narrowness of their own group experience, never reaching out, never learning to celebrate others' differences.[13]

Prior to 1954, segregation and discrimination were legal in the United States, just as apartheid is in South Africa today. In the United States, however, laws were changed to make government-approved discrimination illegal. Unfortunately, laws don't change beliefs. But fairly written, well-enforced laws can make it more difficult for racists to discriminate.

Here is a hypothetical case: A clerk believes minorities are inferior and should not be hired. But she does not have the power to act on her beliefs. If, however, the clerk is promoted to manager, with the power to hire and fire, she will be able to discriminate.

Think about the consequences of people like police officers, real estate agents, judges, principals and loan officers sharing the clerk's beliefs. That is why civil rights laws are important. They help protect minorities from being discriminated against by those in power.

Just as race is not the only criterion for discrimination, superiority is not the only justification for it. For example, nineteenth-century Chinese immigrants were faced with the irrational argument that they were *too* hardworking and *too* diligent to compete with white workers. That same argument is resurfacing today in colleges and universities. While blacks and Hispanics were excluded from the more prestigious universities for years because they were stereotyped as incompetent, today Asian students are criticized for being too industrious, too productive, and too competitive. The great educator and presidential advisor, Mary McLeod Bethune, said it succinctly: "[racism] will use any excuse to excuse itself."

Race hatred often leads to *violence*. People who form paramilitary groups to "defend America from a minority takeover" fall into the category of extremists. There are vigilante gangs in America today who roam the streets meting out a perverse form of "justice" to a whole race by choosing an innocent representative to beat or kill.

According to FBI profiles, such extremists are generally powerless as individuals, so they seek strength in numbers. People with shared hatred gain a pseudopower within the organizational structures of such groups as the neo-Nazis and Ku Klux Klan.

The fact that these groups are motivated by hate and are prone to violence serves as a deterrent to membership. There are people who share the same beliefs as the Klan and neo-Nazis, but they would not join a subversive organization because of their jobs or social status.[14]

Race hatred, permitted to gain unlimited power, will be predictably disastrous. The state-sponsored genocide perpetrated by Nazi Germany is an example of what happens when people who hate gain power.

Hitler's extermination campaign took the lives

of six million human beings for no other reason than they were Jews. It began in little ways . . . an ethnic joke, stereotyping that was never challenged, then restrictions, loss of jobs, loss of civil rights, loss of voting rights, and finally loss of life.

The world was horrified when it saw the survivors of the Nazi concentration camps. Hearts were touched when people read *The Diary of Anne Frank.* Yet, less than forty years after World War II, Florrie Rost Van Tonningen, 74, the widow of a Dutch Nazi leader, was fined $1000 for distributing anti-Semitic pamphlets denying that the Nazis slaughtered millions of Jews. At a reputable American university, a professor wrote a paper stating the Holocaust didn't really happen. Young adults and teenagers are joining neo-Nazi groups and openly wearing swastikas. Jesse Jackson, the first black man to run for president of the United States, referred to New York as "Hymietown," an insulting racial slur.

One of the most startling developments in recent political history was the election of David Duke to the Louisiana House of Representatives in March 1989.

Duke, a silver-tongued orator who cloaks his racism in carefully constructed euphemisms, is a former Grand Wizard of the Ku Klux Klan, and has been photographed wearing a swastika armband. Theodore Ellenoff, president of the American Jewish Committee, had this response to Duke's election: "While there had been significant progress in recent years in containing bigotry in America, this development reminds us that there is much more work to be done." A. I. Botnick, regional director of B'nai B'rith in New Orleans, said, "Duke's election . . . is a gain for the forces of racism and bigotry."[15]

It is important to note that massacres and pogroms were not invented by Hitler. Attempts at genocide have occurred in every corner of the world. History shows us repeatedly what happens when extremists are given the power to carry out their goals.

Play the "what if" game with yourself. What if in the future a radical racist rose to power? What if he or she was articulate, poised, and charismatic? What if this person made promises that would make your life better but at the expense of other Americans? Suppose this person wanted to change the Constitution and reduce the powers of Congress? What if the Supreme Court justices, attorney general, and military chiefs were all hand-picked by this extremist? Where would you stand if this new Hitler targeted one racial group for extermination? These are chilling questions to ponder. Even more unsettling are the possible answers.

MINORITY RESPONSES TO RACISM

Now it is time to look at the other side of racism.

Ask yourself how you might act if throughout childhood you heard repeatedly that your race was nonproductive, lazy, and foolish. And suppose nothing you did could change the opinions others had of you because of your skin color, your religion, your ancestry? Suppose your language or your religion was held up to public ridicule? What attitudes would you have about those who did such a thing?

Victims of prejudice often develop a faulty belief system in the same way children learn to be prejudiced. They learn to protect themselves by building ego defenses essential to their survival. Often these defenses are as irrational and stereotypical as racism itself. Preoccupation is a kind of paranoia that occurs when a people are discriminated against over a long period of time. Preoccupation causes hypersensitivity, a "chip on the shoulder attitude." For example, some black Americans read bigotry into every situation involving a white person. They can rarely have a conversation without referring to "how bad the Man is treating us." Like the boy who cried wolf, these people tend to cry racism and discrimination at the drop of a hat, thus weakening the case against the real wolf—those who are truly guilty.[16]

Aggression against one's own group is another response to persistent rejection. Sociologist Gordon W. Allport stated in *The Nature of Prejudice*, "Class distinctions within groups are often a result of trying to free oneself from responsibility for the handicap which the group as a whole suffers." Allport gave as examples the "Lace Curtain" Irish who looked down on the "Shanty Irish" and Jews of German origin who saw themselves as aristocrats and looked down on East European Jews. Skin color, occupation, and degree of education helped mark the strata among blacks.

Withdrawal, self-hate, and denial of heritage are extreme responses to prejudice. A good example of this is found in the film adaptation of the Broadway play *The Wiz*. Scarecrow (played by Michael Jackson) believed he couldn't climb down off the pole that held him both a physical and mental captive, because he wasn't smart enough. The crows had Scarecrow convinced that "You can't win. You can't break even, and you can't get out of the game." Like the self-fulfilling prophecy that it was, Scarecrow believed, "If you say I will fail, then I will fail."

Drug use, low self-esteem, poor academic achievement, criminal behavior, and other self-destructive forms of despair are the results of mental defeat. If the expectations remain low, so will the results, which only adds fuel to the racist argument, "What more can you expect from *them*."

Anger and hostility are a predictable response to long-term racism and discrimination. But anger is not necessarily negative. For some it can be a motivator, a call to action—positive action. Rev. Dr. Martin Luther King, Jr., was angry about segregation. He believed it to be morally wrong and that it should not be allowed to exist in a democratic society. King directed his anger in positive ways and conducted peaceful demonstrations and nonviolent protests. The results of King's efforts are well known.

Here's another example of channeling anger in positive ways. Many inner-city residents are angry about taking the blame for the condition of their housing. "If tenants owned the property and managed it," says Bertha Gilkey, tenant housing advocate from St. Louis, "things would change." Gilkey believes that tenant management is the key to improving inner-city housing. She also says that enforcement of housing codes, fire ordinances, and better police-community relations would help force absentee landlords to bring their rental property up to standard.[17]

But too many others let their anger lead them

into hostile acts and extremism. Like their bigoted counterparts, these people join hate groups that preach intolerance and advocate violence.

Before his death in 1988, James Baldwin, a great American writer who had taken a stand against intolerance all his life, left the victims of racism some sound advice. "You must always be fair, you must always be balanced, and you must always live like that. Because you don't want to be poisoned inside."[18] You might also consider Professor Allport's eloquent statement: "If we foresee evil in our fellow man, we tend to provoke it; if good, we elicit it."

In the next chapter we'll take a more personal look at racism and discrimination.

THREE

LET'S TALK ABOUT RACISM AND DISCRIMINATION

INCIDENT
by Countee Cullen

Once riding in old Baltimore
Head-filled, heart-filled with glee,
I saw a Baltimorian kept looking
straight at me.
Now I was eight and very small,
but he was no wit bigger,
And so I smiled, but he
Poked out his tongue
and called me "nigger!"
I saw the whole of Baltimore
from May until December.
Of all the things that
happened there,
That's all that I remember.

Thomasina F. Hassler is a high school guidance counselor. Mrs. Hassler and the author led a discussion on racism and discrimination with twenty-five high school students who volunteered to participate. The group discussed how racism and discrimination affected their school environments, their lives, and their future. The students were from varied races, religions, ethnic groups, and from different socio-economic levels.

NAME CALLING
AND RACIAL SLURS

One of the group's major concerns was the cause and effect of racial name calling and put-downs. The group agreed that name calling, like swear words, were weapons used to provoke an argument, get back at a person, or to hurt him. A slur directed at a particular ethnic group was sure to get the desired results in a confrontation: pain, anger, shame, hostility, guilt, and embarrassment. Students admitted that they had used racial slurs when angered. Several students said they told racial jokes and used ethnic names but not with the intent to hurt an individual. "It's kind of the way we talk," they said.

Students talked about how ethnic put-downs made them feel. Many times the discussion was charged with emotion, but every effort was made to keep the conversation open and honest.

The following is an exchange between Debbie and Andre.

DEBBIE: I don't understand what's the big deal. How come some people get so mad about being called names? I mean, everybody

*Talking about feelings regarding
racism and discrimination can help
ease mutual misunderstanding.*

gets called names. Name calling is used just to get a reaction, so why give them the satisfaction of seeing you get all bent out of shape.

ANDRE: That's easy to say. See, I can call you *white trash* all day long, and the words would just bounce right off, because you know it isn't true. You *know* you are somebody, because of the way you live, the clothes you wear and the car you drive. But when somebody calls me *nigger* it's like they're saying, no matter how much we try as a race to do better . . . we'll always be the lowest race. That word lumps us all together. That's why we get mad . . . fight back . . . never let anybody get away with saying it.

DEBBIE: I'm not saying that racial names shouldn't hurt. I know they do. But, why not ignore them? Why let them upset you so much?

ANDRE: Why? Okay, get this one. What do you call the first black president? Answer: Nigger.

DEBBIE: That's tasteless.

ANDRE: Yeah, but a lot of kids thought it was real funny. But the dude who told it . . . I pushed the dude's face in his mashed potatoes; everybody say I was overreacting. I was wearing a "Jesse Jackson for President" button. The joke was not funny to me. It's like I said, no matter what a black person becomes . . . even president of the United States . . . it doesn't change how people think about black people as a whole.

IMAGES

Mrs. Hassler shared her concepts about word images.

"Words give us pictures," she explained, writing *D-O-G* on the chalkboard. "You don't see the letters or the word, you see a picture of that word. And each of us has a different visual." Some stated they saw a brown-and-white spotted dog, while others saw a small tan dog with floppy ears. "Change the word to *collie* and the image dissolves and everybody sees the same breed of dog." Mrs. Hassler followed with *Lassie*, a specific collie with a history. "There is an accumulation of information about Lassie that we all associate with her breed: bravery, loyalty, and honesty."

The students learned that they all have emotional responses to words. "What about *puppy?* There is nothing menacing about a small puppy. Most people smile when they think of a puppy, even those who aren't fond of full-grown dogs. Now, watch what happens to the emotions when the word is shifted to *mad dog*. What would your feelings be if you had been attacked by a dog?" The visual would be frightening.

Behavior problems, slow learners, underprivileged—the visual called up by these phrases far too often is of a minority. Euphemisms like these, combined with racial slurs, jokes, and put-downs, send powerful visuals, accompanied by a long and ugly history, as indicated in the conversation between Andre and Debbie.

"If you can change word pictures," says Mrs. Hassler, "and replace them with positive imaging, then attitudes can be changed, too."

LET'S TALK ABOUT
THE WORD "NIGGER"

No racial name has been more devastating or confusing to a whole race of people than *nigger*. Poets have written about the pain the word causes; comedians have tried to laugh the hurt out of it, but nothing has checked the power of that single word to hold an entire race as psychological hostages. To complicate matters, black people have sent mixed messages regarding their feelings about the word's use and implication. Being called a nigger will send one person into a violent rage, while another person will use it openly in reference to his neighbor.

Mrs. Hassler believes each individual responds to word images and not the word itself. We don't see letters in our head when a word is used, we see the picture of that word. Experiences and values determine how an individual will "see" the word.

"We all learned a long time ago that black is beautiful. Tell me what you see when I say *black*," says Mrs. Hassler.

A night sky . . .
my good stockings . . .
my favorite purse . . .
my hair . . .
my mama . . .

The word *nigger* is a derivative of *niger,* a sixteenth-century Portuguese word meaning black. Slavers called their African captives *nigers* . . . blacks.

It wasn't until after the Civil War that *nigger* took on the powerful imagery that it has today. White supremacists would not accept being equal to black people. They used whatever means they could to keep former slaves at the bottom of the social and economic order.

Up until that time, *nigger* had been a noun, simply describing a person who was a black slave. With the formation of the Ku Klux Klan and other white supremacy groups, *nigger* defined the way a race would be treated for nearly a century. *Nigger* became a verb. It summarized all the ugly ways in which black people were treated: raped, beaten, branded, denied the right to vote, burned out of schools and homes, segregated, lynched. For black people, *nigger* was not just a word but the culmination of their collective suffering.[19]

Whites who were so poor they had to pick cotton in fields alongside blacks had the telltale sign of a sun-burned neck. These lower-class whites were disdainfully called "rednecks," another negative name.

"I'm of Italian descent," said a participant. "Somebody called me *wop,* and I didn't even know I was insulted. What does it mean? Where does it come from?"

The following explanation was given. Some immigrants came into the United States through New Orleans. Many were Italians who did not have proper papers. Until they cleared immigration they were kept on board ship and/or put to work as dock workers. To show that they were legitimate workers they were given WOP badges, the acronym meaning *W*orker *O*n *P*ayroll, or *W*ith*o*ut *P*apers.

"What about *wetbacks?*"

Sometimes Mexicans illegally entering the United States swam across the Rio Grande. If confronted by border guards, they insisted they were Mexican-Americans. So, the guards had a simple test. If the captive's back was wet, the guards assumed the person was a "wetback"—an illegal alien. It is not known what happened to a person caught perspiring.

A reluctant participant asked, "Why do blacks call themselves nigger?"

Julius Lester, in *To Be a Slave,* explains: "[Nigger] was a brutal, violent word that stung the soul of the slave more than the whip did his back. But the slaves took that ugly word and like the white man's religion, made it their own. In their mouths it became an affectionate, endearing word. As much as possible they robbed it of its ability to spiritually maim them."[19]

Slaves established a language of ambiguity. Word meanings changed depending upon the way they were said or pronounced, the gestures that accompanied them, or the context in which they appeared. For example, *bad* can mean "not good," but when pronounced ba-ad, it means "good."

Slaves created this secret communication style so that they could talk to each other in the presence of whites without being understood. For example, a black preacher could praise a runaway by calling him a "ba-ad nigger." The master, having heard this, would interpret the statement literally. But, slaves who understood the coded message interpreted the message just the opposite.

CODE-SWITCHING

KEVIN: Hey, we do that today. You mean the slaves did that? I thought it was just slang.

JACKIE: It's a lot you don't know, Kev.

KEVIN: Shut-up, girl, 'fo I have to smack you.

ANN: Now, are you serious, Kevin? I mean, when you spoke, your words sounded so angry. But you wouldn't really hit Jackie, would you?

KEVIN: Hey, Jackie's a sister. She knows I was just talkin'. That's our way of kiddin' around and stuff. See, if I had said that to you, Ann, you would have got all tight and everything . . . reported me for messing with you, right?

ANN: I guess so . . .

KEVIN: Communication breakdown, right?

Mrs. Hassler introduced the term *code-switching*. "Many black language patterns are holdovers from slavery. One, as we discussed earlier, was the ability to change the meanings of words by the way they were said. Another is code-switching, which is the ability to shift your language pattern to fit the social environment.

"Black people use the language depending upon who they were talking to and about what. What Kevin said to Jackie was coded with a message that she understood to be joking. Ann, who didn't understand the message, misinterpreted Kevin's intent. If Kevin wanted to communicate with Ann he would have to code-switch and use the language differently."[20]

The debate over black language patterns is a very sensitive issue for many people. In April 1989 at Horton Watkins High School in St. Louis, where the student population of 1000 is 28% black, the student newspaper *Panorama* featured an article on black English. The first paragraph of the story began: "I can skate better than Louis, and I only be eight. If you be goin' real fast, you done catched up with him now."

Two students at the school named Eric Rowe and Dominik Lenoir believed the story "implied that all black people spoke in ungrammatical slang." The editor of the newspaper defended the article saying, "The objectors read the headline, the first few lines and blew up." Actually, when the full article was read it was generally laudatory, stating that "blacks should not be criticized for speaking differently."

The principal quickly called an assembly in the school auditorium and let people speak openly about the issue. About 200 students "got their feelings on the floor," said the principal. Lenoir and Rowe came away feeling that the open discussion had been helpful. "I'm glad we talked about it instead of covering it up," said Rowe. "I hope this isn't the end of it. I hope that people take notice of certain things like that blacks and whites sit separately in the student lounge. We have to recognize that people have differences and try to find out what they are." "There is no right or wrong way to communicate," says Mrs. Hassler, "just different ways of using words."

BOY! AND YO' MAMA

The students in Mrs. Hassler's group wanted to know why *boy* was so offensive to black males, and why *yo' mama* almost always caused a fight.

Yo' mama came from a barroom game called "Playing the Dozens," popular about the mid-

1920s, although verbal challenges date back to slavery times. Two men challenged each other to a contest of verbal skill and mental dexterity. Each man had six exchanges (a total of a dozen), all prefaced by "Yo' mama is so ugly . . ." The one-line zingers were usually derogatory, but no offense was taken, because it was a game. The listeners, called *signifiers,* scored each round and a winner was declared.

To play the dozens without permission from both players was considered an insult, and great offense was taken. So *yo' mama* grew into a challenge to fight. In the days of dueling, gentlemen challenged an insult with a slap across the face with gloves. *Yo' mama* carries the same dynamics. To refuse a duel was the height of cowardice. The same psychology exists within the black community.

So when children use *yo' mama,* they are not actually talking about each other's mothers. They are challenging each other to fight. It is a way of antagonizing, setting up a duel.

Historically *boy* was another hurtful word used to keep minorities in their places. Hispanics, Asians, and blacks were all referred to as boys, even if they were grown men with children of their own. When the men were too elderly to be called boys, they were called "Uncle," or "Old Man." (Minority women remained girls until they became "Auntie" or "Old Woman.")[21]

Sometimes in defiance, parents named their sons "Man," or "Sir," to artificially force respect. Of course, a boy is a boy regardless of his race. Jesse Jackson, who often speaks to students, warns that "man" is a title with responsibilities that accompany its use.

HOLLY: Speaking of Jesse Jackson, how do you defend his calling New York "Hymietown." How could he, a person who has been called names and knows how awful it must feel, then turn around and use a racial slur toward another group?

SARAH: I'm Jewish and the first and only other time I heard "Hymietown" was when my father's business partner called New York by that name. It's disgusting, but people use racial terms so offhandedly, they don't really realize what they are saying . . . like my father's partner.

LYONEL: Jesse Jackson was big enough to apologize.

HOLLY: Okay. That's the double standard we've been talking about. If Jesse Jackson can say "Hymietown," then apologize and be forgiven, why can't David Duke, [the Ku Klux Klansman who won a seat in the Louisiana House of Representatives] be accepted? Do you really think blacks are going to trust David Duke? Then why should we trust Jesse Jackson?

LYONEL: Jesse Jackson is a human being, just like you or me. I guess we expect more out of people who are running for public office than is humanly possible sometimes. We have all used racial slurs; that doesn't make them right, but we do use them. He didn't say it in front of a lot of people, he was overheard and quoted by a newspaper reporter. The standards for Jesse Jackson are the same as David Duke. I say judge them both by the things they do.

HOLLY: I think black people want a double standard. If a white person had been overheard using a racial term, he would have been forced to resign. Jackson was not. That's a double standard.

LYONEL: If the voters didn't like what Jesse Jackson said, they had a choice. Don't vote for him. But I think he did okay last time out.

It was generally agreed that name calling and racial put-downs were painful and hurtful regardless of who used them and why. But being able to talk about feelings and ask questions without fear of misunderstanding helped a lot. And at the same time, the discussion raised more questions: Should books that contain racial slurs be banned from the libraries? Should we support comedians who profit by using stereotypical material?

Mrs. Hassler and another high school counselor, Mrs. Lillian Curtis, recognized that there was a need for a program where questions like these and others could be discussed, a program that would also help promote and encourage academic achievement among minority students. So they started the Partners in Achievement at Webster Groves High School in Webster Groves, Missouri. The group meets bi-weekly to hear guest speakers, watch videotapes, take field trips, and have discussions about raising self-esteem and strategies for academic achievement. Groups of this kind are common in school districts nationwide, and in almost all cases the ability to talk, share ideas, and vent frustrations and concerns is helpful. "If we can keep the lines of communication open, then that means progress can be made," says Mrs. Hassler. "Talking is the first step in overcoming the barriers raised by ignorance. I recommend open and honest discussions, like the one we just modeled, to those who are interested in taking a stand against racism and discrimination."

TWENTY PROBLEM ATTITUDES OF BLACK STUDENTS

(From interviews by the authors with black students)

If whitey puts a hand on me I'm gonna do something bad to him. I don't want nobody white to touch me.

I quit trying because the man won't give me a chance.

Black students can't cooperate with one another.

There is no way a white teacher can teach me a thing about being black. . . . Nothing!

All white people are prejudiced against blacks, no matter what they try to do to cover it up.

I can't do the amount of work they expect me to do and hang out at the same time.

In order to make it you have to turn your back on blackness and be like them (whites), then you have a better chance.

I have to be like the rest of the black students or I'll be an outcast.

Being black means being like Africans.

White people owe us because of what they did to the slaves.

My mama told me not to take no stuff off of no white teachers or kids. She'll come up to the school in a minute and set everybody straight.

The white man's education, religion, and social structure don't include blacks and there is no way we fit into the picture.

I don't know why he's [a black student] running for Student Council President. He doesn't have a chance. I'm not even going to vote, because what good will it do.

They [whites] should just let us black kids do our thing and leave us alone.

All I need is some smoke and my box and the rest of it can go . . .

In order for blacks to make it we have to be better than they are three times over.

The black teachers—or the ones the white people hire—are out of touch. They aren't black anymore but black-white people.

White people are scared to death of blacks and I use it to get away with all kind of stuff.

All my friends are white. I am totally accepted and have no problems.

Being black and a woman is probably the worst thing in the world. What chance do we have?

TWENTY PROBLEM ATTITUDES
OF WHITE TEACHERS

*(From interviews by the authors
with white classroom teachers)*

Surprisingly, some of the nicest students I have are black.

I just love all my students. Every year at the end of school I have a big picnic at my farm and I have all the kids out, including the black kids.

We allow our minority students to be late for school, because they're lucky to get here at all, given the home situation.

The highest score on the math test was made by Charles, a black boy who lives down in the projects.

We don't have teacher home visits any longer because, well, you know, some of the families live in the projects and we couldn't ask our women teachers to go there at night.

We go out of our way to make sure our black students get a fair shake.

We have a colored woman who works in our cafeteria and she is the nicest lady you'd ever want to meet. She just tickles me to death, the way she puts those bad black kids in their place.

Black students are so loud.

Blacks are the best athletes. It's their only way out.

What do black people want?

This used to be a nice place to teach but *now* it has really changed since. . .

The best way to handle black kids is to be tough, no exceptions.

The best way to handle black kids is to be tolerant; poor things; they need understanding.

I teach in the inner-city schools because I want to do something to help blacks get out of the ghetto and improve their lives.

I just about have my black kids to the point where they act like the other kids.

I say, those (blacks) who want to learn and act like human beings, let 'em stay, but those who don't, let 'em get out.

The white students are scared to death of the black students.

I see kids as kids, black, white, red, or yellow, no difference whatsoever.

I'm so tired of all this special treatment black people get. I'm so sick of guidelines, Federal programs, and assistance. That's the problem—we give them too much.

Things aren't what they should be (at our school) but we're better than most (schools).

====FOUR====

RACE ISSUES AND
THE AMERICAN GOVERNMENT:
FROM 1776 TO THE PRESENT

There is hardly an American who would not agree with Judge Learned Hand's definition of liberty as "the spirit which seeks to understand the minds of other men and women." But, when Judge Hand delivered his eloquent address, entitled "The Spirit of Liberty," in 1944, black Americans were defending democracy—fighting and dying in segregated military units. Japanese-Americans had been rounded up and held in internment camps and their property confiscated without due process of law. Although America was a democratic country, the government tolerated racism and discrimination. The United States Constitution, though very specific about the rights guaranteed to all citizens, is subject to interpretation. That is why government-sponsored racism and discrimination were allowed to exist within a democracy almost from the beginning of this nation.

FROM THE BEGINNING

While the American revolutionaries were fighting for their own freedom and rights, they made certain that the human rights of another people were systematically denied. In so doing, they established a dual system of government-sponsored discrimination on one hand and democracy for white men on the other. (Women and other minorities were also excluded from government participation at that time.)

The first draft of the Declaration of Independence contained this statement:

> *[King George] has waged cruel war against human nature itself, violating its most sacred rights of life and liberty in the persons of a distant people who never offended him, capturing and carrying them into slavery in another hemisphere, or to incur miserable death in their transportation thither.*[23]

When Thomas Jefferson submitted the draft to the Continental Congress, the southern delegation objected. They feared the strong antislavery language might make it more difficult to continue slavery once the ties to England were ended. Thomas Jefferson agreed reluctantly to delete the statement from the final draft of the Declaration of Independence. The first document of the revolutionary government was thus tainted by racism.[23]

When the Revolution ended, a new nation was born. The leaders had the weighty task of forming a real government. The world was watching the fledgling nation with interest. After much debate, it was decided a constitutional government would work best. But getting representatives from the thirteen uniquely different states to agree on anything was a difficult task—if not altogether impossible. While the colonists had been united in their efforts against England, in freedom the thirteen states were suspicious of a central government. They feared losing their independence.

Nevertheless, a Constitutional Convention was called in the summer of 1786, and representatives came together to shape America's future. One of the most hotly debated issues at the convention was slavery. Where would the new government stand with regard to it?

SLAVERY AND THE CONSTITUTION

The decisions made at the Constitutional Convention regarding slaves have had far-reaching ramifications upon our lives today, and no doubt some may be carried into the twenty-first century.

Some delegates wanted to abolish slavery and be rid of it forever. The unified southern delegates threatened to walk out if any such idea was considered. Through a series of concessions made to the pro-slavery delegates, the United States Constitution referred to slaves as something less than full human beings. Trying to overcome that general concept has been a two-hundred-year struggle for black Americans.[23]

It began when the South wanted to count the slaves when appointing representatives based on population, but not when fixing their share of taxation. It was agreed that a slave would be counted as "three-fifths" of a person when appointing representatives and assessing taxes.

Some delegates were vehemently opposed to the concession. James Wilson, one of the key framers of the Constitution, was most vocal. He asked, "Are [slaves] admitted as citizens? Then why are they not admitted on an equality with white citizens." His objections did not change the course of events.

Then again, article I, section 9, clause 1 of the Constitution states that "migration and importation of slaves into the existing states will be legal until 1808." Article IV, section 2, clause 3 states that runaway slaves were to be returned upon request of the master.

James Madison, often called the "Father of the Constitution," was strongly against slavery, but realized that without making compromises with the South, the Constitution would not be ratified. Yet he went on record in protest against the continuation of slave trade until 1808. "Twenty years," he said, "will produce all the mischief that can be apprehended from the liberty to import slaves . . . It is to be hoped that by expressing a national disapprobation of this trade we may destroy it, and save ourselves from reproaches, and our posterity the imbecility ever attendant on a country filled with slaves."[23]

CONSTITUTIONAL INTERPRETATIONS

The Constitution was ratified in June 1788. It helped establish a strong central government, but each state also had a constitution. In the southern states "slave codes" were instituted to further protect the property interests of slave owners. Slaves were considered "property," but that concept was challenged in the Supreme Court in 1857. Chief Justice Roger B. Taney, a southern Democrat, presented the court's decision in the historic *Dred Scott* case. A majority of the sitting Supreme Court Justices were southerners. They ruled that Dred Scott, a slave, was not entitled to freedom because he had lived away from his master in a free state.

The well-known *Dred Scott* decision reduced human beings to the level of sheep and cattle, and in Justice Taney's words, slaveholders had "the rights to traffic in it, like an ordinary article of merchandise and property was guaranteed to the citizens of the United States." The court went on to say that black people were not intended to be included as citizens under the Constitution but "were regarded as beings of an inferior order . . . altogether unfit to associate with the white race, either in social or political relations; and so far inferior, that they had no rights which the white man was bound to respect."[23]

Freedom, justice, and equality were not new ideas, created for the sole purpose of a few privileged people. So, it wasn't long before people of this nation pushed to end slavery. The North and South were at odds on the issue and war was inevitable.

In 1863, in the heat of the Civil War, President Abraham Lincoln issued the Emancipation Proclamation freeing the slaves in all rebel states. Historian and writer Lerone Bennett called the document "dry and matter-of-fact in its approach," lacking the typical Lincoln eloquence found, for example, in the Gettysburg Address. The long-awaited, long-fought-for proclamation simply said, "And by virtue of the power [invested in me] I do order and declare that all persons held as slaves within said designated States, and parts of States, are, and henceforward shall be free; and that the Executive government of the United States . . . will recognize and maintain the freedom of said persons." Thus the United States government freed four million men, women, and children of color from human bondage.

The physical chains had been broken, but the mental bonds remained on master as well as slave. Whites were taught from childhood that they were superior. Blacks were taught from childhood that they were incapable of thinking or doing anything worthwhile except serve others. How could a piece of paper change generations of conditioning? It was as difficult for the slave to think of himself as equal to his former master as it was for the master to accept a slave as his equal.[24]

THE RECONSTRUCTION LAWS

Although George Washington called the United States Constitution the "precious depository of American happiness," the freedoms and promises the document guaranteed were not applicable to African-Americans, women, and other minorities at the time of its ratification.

But even then, the framers of the Constitution were not so impudent as to believe the document they had written was infallible. They were far-sighted enough to realize that unforeseen conditions would make it necessary to amend the document—not easily, and not at the whim of a few people, yet still possible. Thomas Jefferson noted that "The Constitution belongs to the living, not the dead."

The first test of the amendment system came when the first ten amendments—the Bill of Rights—were added to the Constitution in 1791. After the Civil War the Reconstruction amendments helped to nullify the concessions the framers of the Constitution had made on the issue of slavery.[25]

The Thirteenth, Fourteenth, and Fifteenth Amendments were the government's way of taking a firm position against reenslavement, and for voting rights and individual freedoms. Congress tried to establish the framework of justice in the federal system and provide protection for the freedmen against state actions.

The Thirteenth Amendment abolished slavery in the United States forever. The Fourteenth Amendment limited the power of states to pass discriminatory laws, stating "No state shall make or enforce any law which shall abridge the privileges or immunities of citizens of the United States, nor shall any State deprive any person of life, liberty, or property without due process of law; nor deny to any person within its jurisdiction the equal protection of the laws."

The Fourteenth Amendment provided the freedmen with the protection against states passing laws that were in conflict with the Constitution.

The Fifteenth Amendment gave black men the right to vote: "The right of the citizens of the United States to vote shall not be denied or abridged by the United States or by any State on

During reconstruction, many blacks were
elected to state legislatures throughout
the South. Later in the century, passage
of repressive laws sharply limited black
participation in government.

account of race, color, or previous condition of servitude."

In addition to the three constitutional amendments, Congress also passed The Civil Rights Bill of 1875, stating that "All persons within the jurisdiction of the United States shall be entitled to the full and equal enjoyment of the accommodations, advantages, facilities, and privileges of inns, public conveyances on land or water, theaters, and other places of public amusement; subject only to the conditions and limitations established by law and applicable alike to citizens of every race and color, regardless of any previous condition of servitude."[26]

The Constitution clearly outlined the rights and privileges of all citizens regardless of color. If the freedmen had been able to move freely within American society—working, learning, living life with all the advantages others had—the present-day situation might be very different. Unfortunately, the Constitution is subject to interpretation, and Supreme Court decisions are only as honorable as those men and women who interpret them.

Briefly, this is what happened between 1875 and 1900. After a cooling-off period, the wounds opened during the North–South conflict began to heal. According to Lerone Bennett, "So long as blacks posed no threat to the political and economic supremacy of whites, people were content to live with them on terms of relative intimacy. But when [blacks] became citizens, when they got ballots in their hands and pencils and paper, there were demands for laws and arrangements that would humiliate them and keep them in their place."

By the late 1890s attitudes had changed. Officials were elected who wanted a more decentralized government, in which states handled issues concerning education, housing, employment, and public accommodations. State legislatures began passing laws that interfered with black people's right to vote. For example, in some southern states, laws were passed that prevented a person from registering to vote unless his grandfather had voted. Since most blacks at that time had grandfathers who had been slaves and unable to vote, this eliminated a large number of the black voting population. Although these "grandfather clauses" were clearly in violation of the Fifteenth Amendment to the Constitution, the Supreme Court ruled that the state laws were not unconstitutional because they applied to everybody and did not single out blacks.

Once again governmental officials used their power to interpret the Constitution based on their own prejudices. In this way African-Americans and other minorities lost their freedoms one by one. With popular opinion against them and no political muscle with which to fight back, the freedmen lost all the gains they had won since the war.

PLESSY V. FERGUSON

The most devastating decision and the deathblow to civil rights and equality in this country came with the infamous *Plessy* v. *Ferguson* decision of 1896.

Once again the Supreme Court was packed with southern justices. They upheld a Louisiana law that required railroad companies to provide "separate but equal" accommodations for whites and blacks. The court ruled that the Fourteenth

Amendment was not intended "to abolish distinctions based upon color, or to enforce social as distinguished from political equality or a commingling of the two races upon terms unsatisfactory to either."[27]

Note the wording of the Supreme Court: "We consider the underlying fallacy of the plaintiff's argument to consist in the assumption that the enforced separation of the two races stamps the colored race with a badge of inferiority. If this be so, it is not by reason of anything found in the act but solely because the colored race chooses to put that construction to it."

When black leaders of the day called the decision discriminatory, they were accused of being reactionary and militant. Justice Harlan, who wrote the court's only dissenting opinion, recognized the "bankruptcy in the court's reasoning." He knew a loophole had been found that would permit southern states to pass state laws that would discriminate against people of color, and the federal government was promising not to interfere.

Justice Harlan noted that the *real* meaning of the ruling was "that colored citizens cannot be allowed to sit in public coaches occupied by white citizens." He warned that if other states were permitted to enact similar laws, "the effect would be the highest degree of mischief. States would have the power to interfere with the full enjoyment of the blessings of freedom; to regulate civil rights common to all citizens, upon the basis of race; and to place in a condition of legal inferiority a large body of American citizens."[28]

The fears of Justice Harlan were soon realized. By the turn of the twentieth century the United

States was a segregated nation, which it justified with the "separate but equal" interpretation of the Fourteenth Amendment.

Jim Crow laws were quickly passed all over the South and in the West. Asian-Americans, Hispanics, and Native Americans were also forced to endure segregation by law. The outcome was a totally segregated society.

Blacks were locked outside of the mainstream of American life. People of color were denied the right to vote, forbidden to serve on juries, and denied entry into white-owned theaters, restaurants, hotels, and inns. Under President Woodrow Wilson federal government buildings were segregated in Washington, D.C. Desks of black employees were curtained off; separate bathrooms and separate tables in the cafeterias were provided.

Having to live under such adverse social and political conditions made some blacks angry and bitter. Sometimes this frustration led to riots. Racial harmony, as hoped for by Reconstructionists, seemed a far-fetched idea. During the summer of 1919, called "Red Summer," blacks were lynched, burned, tarred and feathered for "gettin' out of place!"

Segregation had negative effects on whites as well. In 1931 H.L. Mencken and Charles Angoff ran a two-part series in *American Mercury* magazine ranking the states from good to bad. Their criteria included wealth, literacy, education, entries in *Who's Who in America,* symphony orchestras, crime, voter registration, infant mortality, transportation, and availability of medical services. Mississippi, the most segregated state in the nation, ranked the lowest, followed by Alabama. In 1972, the survey was run again and Mississippi and Alabama were still at the bottom, further confirmation of Jesse Jackson's belief that "in order to keep black people in the gutter, the white man had to be there himself to make sure the other guy didn't get out."[29]

The enforced segregation of the races continued until the middle of the twentieth century. Then small signs of progress toward equalization began. President Franklin Delano Roosevelt and First Lady Eleanor Roosevelt led the way by including blacks in White House functions and appointing them to decision-making positions. Mary McLeod Bethune served as special advisor on minority affairs to FDR and was a frequent visitor to the White House. After Roosevelt's death, President Harry S. Truman continued taking a stand against discrimination. Against the advice of Generals Dwight Eisenhower and Douglas MacArthur, President Truman ordered that the military be integrated in 1948.

BROWN V. BOARD OF EDUCATION OF TOPEKA, 1954

Earl Warren was appointed Chief Justice of the Supreme Court by President Eisenhower in 1953. Up until that time, Warren had not been recognized as a civil rights liberal. But when a school desegregation case was presented to the Court by the National Association for the Advancement of Colored People (NAACP), Warren agreed to hear it.

In 1954, the Supreme Court heard the *Brown* v. *Board of Education* case. Representing Brown in the case was Thurgood Marshall, then director of

*Army personnel patrolling school grounds
of Little Rock Central High School during
fifties desegregation controversy.*

NAACP's Legal Defense and Educational Fund. On May 17, 1954, the Supreme Court re-interpreted the Fourteenth Amendment and struck down the 1896 *Plessy* v. *Ferguson* decision. The opinion of the Court, read by Chief Justice Earl Warren, stated: "Does segregation of children in public schools solely on the basis of race, even though the physical facilities and other 'tangible' factors may be equal, deprive the children of the minority group of equal educational opportunities? We believe that it does."

"Separate" was "unequal" in the eyes of the Supreme Court, and school desegregation was ordered. "We cannot turn the clock back to 1868, when the [Fourteenth] Amendment was adopted, or even to 1896, when *Plessy* versus *Ferguson* was written . . . but the doctrine of 'separate but equal' has no place." Twelve million children were affected. In border states such as Kansas, Missouri, and Oklahoma, schools were integrated quickly. It was a milestone in the struggle against discrimination in this country. But it did not do a thing to curb racism.[30]

In fact, the South responded with rage. Officials refused to integrate schools. Senators, congressmen, governors, mayors, and school superintendents openly promised to defy the law. Private schools sprung up like mushrooms. Mississippi circuit court judge Tom Brady seemed to represent the overall southern resistance to the Supreme Court decision. In his book *Black Monday*, Brady wrote: "We say to the Supreme Court and to the northern world . . . we have, through our forefathers, died before for our sacred principles. We can, if necessary, die again."[31]

When black children tried to attend formerly all-white schools, they were stoned, spat upon, cursed, and mocked. The National Guard had to be called in to protect students in Arkansas and other southern states. If leaders had acted responsibly and encouraged their constituents to follow the law, things might have been different. Leadership can make a difference. When a young man entered the scene who challenged the imagination and spirit of all Americans, things changed. President John F. Kennedy, a young Eastern liberal, called for an end to racial intolerance. He asked Americans to rise above petty bigotry and the decadence of hatred. Kennedy backed up his rhetoric with action. He asked Congress to draft civil rights legislation and he pushed for better enforcement of existing laws.

The nation responded with the historic civil rights movement of the 1960s. Black and white students, following the model set by Rev. Dr. Martin Luther King, Jr., held peaceful sit-ins, protest marches, rallies, and demonstrations at segregated hotels, theaters, restaurants, and businesses.

For the first time in recent history, black and white Americans were coming together to tear down the walls that separated them. Nobody expected the process to be easy. But the resistance against the idea of racial equality was totally unexpected.

Robert F. Kennedy, the Attorney General, used the full power of his office to protect and defend the rights of all American citizens. Yet, law enforcement officers turned hoses on peaceful demonstrators; three young men were brutally murdered in Mississippi because they had come to help black people register to vote; a Michigan

Leaders of the sixties civil rights movement, including Martin Luther King, Jr., link arms in the landmark March on Washington in August 1963.

housewife was shot and killed because she participated in a march along an Alabama highway.[32]

THE GREAT SOCIETY
OF LYNDON B. JOHNSON

In an eloquent commencement address at Howard University in 1965, President Lyndon B. Johnson expressed the need for government-sponsored programs he would later call "The War on Poverty."

> *You do not wipe away the scars of centuries by saying: Now you are free to go where you want, to do as you desire, and choose the leader you please . . . You do not take a person who for years has been hobbled by chains and liberate him, bring him up to the starting line of a race and then say, "you are free to compete" and still justly believe that you have been completely fair.*

Johnson's War on Poverty was part of his vision of a "Great Society." The results of the War on Poverty are best demonstrated in three key areas:

1. Affirmative action policies aimed at increasing minority participation in higher education and employment;

2. Court decisions and government enforcement action to reduce racial isolation in public schools;

3. Programs designed to upgrade the educational and job skills of poor people, particularly minorities.

What Johnson's Great Society attempted to do was give minorities an *opportunity* to succeed—a "genuine chance to develop one's skills and to reap the rewards of using one's skills." But like the Reconstruction years, a backlash followed in the 1970s.[33]

WHITE BACKLASH

The social programs of the Johnson administration were overshadowed by the Vietnam War. With the election of Richard M. Nixon in 1968, the country took a step toward conservatism—less government, a return to states' rights, and less taxes. Eliot Janeway, a syndicated columnist, used the term "backlash" to describe the reaction of whites who found themselves in direct conflict with blacks for jobs.[34]

The trend toward conservatism (less government) continued throughout the 1970s, and in 1980 voters elected Ronald Reagan president. Reagan set the tone for his administration when he stated (during a debate with President Jimmy Carter during the 1980 campaign) that he was unaware there was a race problem in this country. One of the most charismatic presidents in the modern era, Reagan could make a perfectly foolish statement like this and get away with it.

Many blacks and whites believe that old prejudices have surfaced during the 1980s. The reasons vary. Urban League President John Jacob blames the "resurgence of racist feelings and continued illegal discrimination" on the Reagan administration's "efforts to give tax exempt status to segregated schools, its fight against extension of the civil rights law, its efforts to undermine affirmative action, to destroy the Civil Rights Commission, to stack the courts with right wingers, and its support of South Africa's apartheid government."[5]

Police restrain white students after the
arrival of a busload of black students at
South Boston High School. Desegregation
of the school had been ordered by a court.
In the late sixties and early seventies, a
serious white "backlash" occurred in response
to the success of the civil rights agenda.

Ronald Reagan cannot be singled out as the sole perpetrator of racism and discrimination. However, Joseph Cooper, head of the office of Federal Contract Compliance Programs and one of the highest-ranking blacks in the Reagan administration, stated in his resignation that "there are those who feel they can get away with [racism] because of their perception of the Reagan administration."

Albert Camarillo of Stanford University summarized the effects of the Reagan years on youth. "[College students] have been raised in an era when equal opportunity has been questioned. They have heard people ask if we've done too much for minorities. The Reagan years provided the context that made people feel more comfortable expressing intolerance."

What can be done to stop racism? A famous document from the Johnson era, called the Kerner Report, stated that there must be strategies for action that can produce progress and "make good the promises of American democracy to all citizens—urban and rural, white and black, Spanish surname, American Indians and every minority."

There are very few people who would disagree with that statement. But as long as it is simply read and talked about, it remains little more than idealistic rhetoric unless people, taking their cue from great figures of the past, act decisively to combat racism and discrimination.

FIVE

LEADERS PAST AND PRESENT

Resistance to racism has taken many forms. Nat Turner led a slave revolt, and Harriet Tubman led fellow slaves to freedom along the Underground Railroad. Abolitionist and journalist Elijah Lovejoy of Alton, Illinois, died when his newspaper office was burned by pro-slavery sympathizers. And Frederick Douglass escaped to freedom and used his masterful voice to be an outspoken opponent of slavery.

Early antislavery leaders believed that once slavery was ended the race issue would cease to be a problem. But emancipation only intensified racism, and discrimination became worse than ever.

Except for a brief period after the Civil War, blacks really never experienced equality. Below the Mason-Dixon line, whites fiercely rejected the idea of black equality. Fueled by fear and misconceptions, basically sensible people joined groups like the Ku Klux Klan and other hate groups. The intent was to "save America for white people." The Klan stood as judge and jury when dealing with blacks, Jews, Catholics, and anybody who was "dif-

*Left: A black man lynched for
allegedly raping a white woman
in West Virginia, about 1880*

*Above: An anti-lynching parade in
Washington, D.C., in 1922*

ferent," and meted out justice accordingly. This created a climate in which, according to Ida B. Wells, a black journalist, 10,000 people were lynched in America from 1878 to 1898: an incredible number.[35]

BOOKER T. WASHINGTON VS. W.E.B. DU BOIS

Booker T. Washington and W.E.B. Du Bois led two different movements in the struggle against racism and discrimination in America. When Frederick Douglass died in 1895, there was a black leadership void. For years Douglass had single-handedly crushed every negative stereotype associated with African-Americans—stupidity, laziness, nonproductivity, and dishonesty. Douglass had taught himself to read and write; he was a successful businessman and journalist, and he served as a statesman and diplomat. Douglass was the standard by which all other leaders were measured.

Atlanta hosted the Cotton States' Exposition in 1895. There was a large parade and huge crowds gathered to hear the speeches. The governor had

When Booker T. Washington (1856– 1915) advised blacks to "cast down your buckets where you are," he was accused of advocating complacency.

invited Booker T. Washington, the principal of Tuskegee Institute in Alabama, to give a speech. It was the first time a black had been invited to speak before a white southern audience.

Washington addressed the mostly white crowd on September 18, 1895. He was described by the *New York World* reporter James Creelman as "tall, bony, straight as a Sioux chief, high forehead, straight nose, heavy jaws, and strong, determined mouth." Washington *apologized* for his black brothers' impatience regarding equality, and suggested that his people would prosper best if they took jobs in agriculture, education, and domestic service. Then Washington used a metaphor to state his position on integration. He described two ships passing at the mouth of the Amazon River. The captain of the first ship called for water, and the captain of the second ship answered, "Cast down your buckets where you are." Three times the captains engaged in this dialogue. The narrator continued, explaining that blacks should cast their buckets down where they were by starting at the bottom of the ladder and working up. To whites he said cast your buckets down among "the most patient, faithful, law-abiding, and unresentful people that the world has ever seen."

Washington spread his hands apart. He said, "We can be as separate as the fingers in all things social." Then he made a fist. "Yet," he continued, "one as the hand in all things essential to mutual progress." He concluded, "The wisest among my race understand that the agitation of questions of social equality is the extremist error and that progress in the employment of all the privileges that will come to us must be the result of severe and constant struggles rather than artificial forcing."

When Washington finished, the all-white crowd waved handkerchiefs, hats were tossed in the air, and according to one reporter, "the fairest women of Georgia stood up and cheered." Why were they cheering so madly? Booker T. Washington had essentially said segregation of the races was not a bad thing. His finger-fist analogy was another way of supporting the "separate but equal" loophole southerners were using to deny blacks their constitutional rights. To have a black man seemingly support this idea was more than they had expected.

White leaders immediately proclaimed Washington *the* spokesperson for all black people. Debate over Washington's speech has gone on for decades. Did his position help or hurt?

Given the situation in the South at the time Washington made his "compromise" speech, he did what he thought was best. And money poured into his college. By playing the passive role, Washington appealed to northern philanthropists. Millions of dollars were provided for black education throughout the South with funds and grants from America's richest men and women.

Silently and slowly black youth were educated. Black colleges flourished, and graduates in science, education, agriculture, medicine, law, and business increased. Through education blacks were becoming stronger and better prepared to take a unified stance against racism and discrimination in the future.

But there were other black leaders who resented Washington's philosophy of gradualism. The most vocal opponent was W.E.B. Du Bois. Unlike Washington, Du Bois was the grandson and son of free men and women. He was born in Massachusetts and educated at Fisk and Harvard, earning a Ph.D. in sociology in 1895.

Du Bois was teaching at Atlanta University when Washington gave his speech. Having grown up in an integrated society and never having been held back because of his skin color, Du Bois was intolerant of racism and discrimination. He responded to Washington's address by writing *Souls of Black Folks*. "Mr. Washington distinctly asks that black people give up, at least for the present, three things: First, political power. Second, insistence on civil rights. Third, higher education of Negro youth." Du Bois insisted that black people had three goals: the right to vote, civil equality, and the education of youth according to ability.

Du Bois moved and spoke quickly, like a man with something to do and not enough time to do it. His words were forceful, often angry but compassionate. As far as Du Bois was concerned, there was only one way to obtain justice and equality: "Resist! Resist!" That cry was a frequent conclusion to his stirring speeches.

Booker T. Washington died of a heart attack on November 14, 1915. The stand he took against racism was one of quiet acquiescence. Du Bois chose direct confrontation: attacking injustice by calling attention to it. Theirs were two unique leadership styles, but each was effective in its own way, especially in the historical context in which these two men lived.[36]

THE NATIONAL ASSOCIATION
FOR THE ADVANCEMENT
OF COLORED PEOPLE (NAACP)

There was a race riot in Springfield, Illinois, in 1908. Angry whites flogged and lynched blacks within sight of Lincoln's grave, and shouted "Lincoln freed you, but we'll show you your place."

In response to the riot, a group of whites opposed to racism called a meeting in the "spirit of the abolitionist." On February 12, 1909, the hundredth anniversary of Abraham Lincoln's birth, Bishop Alexander Walters; Oswald Garrison Villard, grandson of William Lloyd Garrison, the great abolitionist; Mary White Ovington, a social worker; and William Walling, a radical white Kentuckian, met to express their growing sense of outrage at the treatment of African-Americans. They called for a national meeting, and W.E.B. Du Bois was invited to attend.[37]

This is an excerpt from the call:

> *If Mr. Lincoln could revisit the country in the flesh . . . he would learn that the Supreme Court, according to the official statement of one of its own judges in the Berea College case, has laid down the principle that if an individual state chooses, it may 'make it a crime for white and colored persons to frequent the same marketplace at the same time, or appear in an assemblage of citizens convened to consider questions of a public or political nature in which all citizens without regard to race are equally interested.' In many states Lincoln would find justice enforced,*

if at all, by judges elected by one element in a community to pass upon the liberties and lives of another. He would see the black men and women, for whose freedoms a hundred thousand soldiers gave their lives, set apart in trains, and segregated in railway stations and in places of entertainment; he would observe that state after state declines to do its elementary duty in preparing the Negro through education.[37]

On May 30, 1909, an interracial group of three hundred met in New York. At a second conference, on May 10, 1910, a permanent organization was created known as the National Association for the Advancement of Colored People. Moorfield Storey, a Boston lawyer, was elected president. The only black officer was Du Bois, who became director of research and publicity. He was also made the editor of NAACP's *Crisis* magazine.

The goal of the NAACP was to use education, persuasion, and negotiation to take a stand against racism and discrimination in America. The NAACP took an active part in fighting discrimination in the courts. Other civil rights organizations would be formed, and other ethnic groups would organize using the NAACP as a model. The NAACP would be the leading advocate against discrimination for half a century.

MARCUS GARVEY AND THE "BACK TO AFRICA" MOVEMENT

Some blacks felt their situation in the United States was hopeless, and the only way to have peace, freedom, or justice was to leave—return to Africa.

Marcus Garvey (1887–1940) wearing the elaborate uniform of his Universal Improvement Association. Garvey was an early black nationalist.

The idea of blacks abandoning America and returning to Africa was not a new one. In 1817, Robert Finley founded the American Colonization Society with the purpose of returning freed slaves to Africa. The organization was supported by both slaves and whites, and in 1822 the society began transporting blacks to what was to become the Republic of Liberia on the West African coast. By 1847 eleven thousand American-born blacks had resettled there.[43]

The idea really didn't catch hold, however, because most Americans of African descent, in spite of their abusive treatment, felt more American than they did African. They had helped found, build, and defend the United States. The idea of leaving it to embrace a whole new culture and life-style was not so easy to accept.

In 1920, Marcus Garvey, a Jamaican man of the people, came on the scene and captured the hearts and minds of many. His approach to combating racism and discrimination was "Do for yourself." Garvey, a dynamic and convincing speaker, was the first leader of prominence to advocate black awareness and self pride among the poor and underprivileged. He told uneducated slum dwellers that they should "clean up and stand up!" His Universal Improvement Association (UIA) headquartered in Harlem, called for black people to emigrate to Africa.

Garvey's plan was bold, his leadership fresh and flashy. His following swelled to the tens of thousands. But in June 1925, Garvey was convicted of mail fraud and sentenced to five years in prison. Later he was exiled. Until his death in 1940, Garvey maintained his innocence and his supporters believed his conviction was political.

Although Garvey's "Back to Africa" movement was never realized, he planted the seeds of pride and self-determination in the hearts and minds of thousands.[40]

OTHER LEADERSHIP MODELS

There are many ways to take a stand. Carter G. Woodson, called the father of black history, saw that textbooks excluded the contributions made by black Americans, so he wrote several volumes of African-American history. He initiated the observance of Negro History Week in 1926, and thanks to his efforts, the American story is more accurate and complete. The 1920s also produced other excellent writers, including poets Langston Hughes, Countee Cullen, and Claude McKay.

A. Philip Randolph, called the father of the black labor movement, headed the Brotherhood of Sleeping Car Porters, the first black union to challenge a major corporation and win. Randolph met with President Franklin D. Roosevelt to discuss the exclusion of black workers in the defense industry. Randolph believed that the government was subsidizing discrimination and threatened to lead a massive protest march on Washington, D.C. As a direct result of Randolph's protest, Roosevelt issued Executive Order No. 8802, which established the Fair Employment Practices Committee. Employers and unions were required to "provide for the full and equitable participation of all workers in defense industries without discrimination because of race, creed, color, or national origin."

Olympic athlete Jesse Owens helped to shatter Adolf Hitler's Aryan supremacy claims by winning three gold medals in the 1936 Olympic Games in Berlin. Ralph J. Bunche, director of the United Nations Trusteeship Division, won the 1950 Nobel Peace Prize for successfully mediating the Palestine conflict, proving to the world that men of color could be world leaders if given a chance.

Thurgood Marshall was one of the NAACP lawyers who presented the *Brown* v. *Board of Education* case to the Supreme Court in 1954. He was appointed to the Supreme Court by President Lyndon Johnson in 1967, the first black man to be appointed to the highest court in the land. Marshall, who still serves on the court, believes "the United States Constitution was designed for the least as well as the greatest Americans."[41]

GIANTS OF THE 1960s
CIVIL RIGHTS MOVEMENT

Rosa Parks was not a lawyer, writer, historian, sociologist, or labor leader. She was a seamstress who worked in a downtown department store in Montgomery, Alabama. Like most people in her socioeconomic bracket, she rode the bus to and from work.

On December 1, 1955, Mrs. Parks paid her fare and, as required by law, took a seat in the black section at the rear of the bus. Later along the route, the bus filled up and Mrs. Parks was expected to give her seat to a white person. She refused and was arrested.

Later that evening, local NAACP leaders and black preachers met to discuss a bus boycott. They selected Rev. Dr. Martin Luther King, Jr., the new

Members of the Warren Supreme Court in 1967. Newly sworn-in Justice Thurgood Marshall, an attorney in the Brown v. Board of Education *case and the first black to serve on the high bench, stands in the second row at right.*

black pastor of Dexter Avenue Baptist Church, to be their leader. He insisted that the demonstration and the boycott had to be nonviolent. "We will win, because our cause is just," he said. And King was right.

The Montgomery Bus Boycott became a milestone in the struggle for freedom and justice. In the end the boycotters helped fulfill the dreams of Douglass, Washington, Du Bois, and all the others who had come before them.[42]

In 1960, three students at North Carolina A&T University also decided to take a stand. First they discussed the absurdity of the segregation system. Their money was good enough to purchase goods in a store, yet they were not permitted to sit at the store's lunch counter and purchase a cup of coffee and a donut. The students decided to challenge the system.

The next day, the students entered Woolworth's and bought a few items and paid for them. Then they proceeded to the lunch counter and, defying the "whites only" sign, they took seats and ordered. The waitress rushed away to get the manager, who told the students blacks could not be served at the lunch counters.

The students kept their seats until the store closed. The following day they returned and once again asked for service. Other students—white and black—joined them, and the community supported them by boycotting the downtown shopping district.

After months of protests and boycotts, the Greensboro merchants and business leaders were on the verge of economic disaster. The stores gave in to the demonstrators' demands; lunch counters

*"Freedom Riders" participating in a sit-in
in the "whites only" section of the
waiting room at the Trailways bus station in
Montgomery, Alabama, in 1961. Through
their efforts, the station was integrated.*

were integrated and a short time later, so were movies, hotels, and restaurants.

What followed next is well known. White and black youth held peaceful sit-in demonstrations all over the South, and accomplished what their elders could not and would not do. They took a stand against institutionalized racism and discrimination and helped revolutionize America's social structure.

The Southern Christian Leadership Conference (SCLC), headed by Dr. King, and the Student Nonviolent Coordinating Committee (SNCC) were the two organizations that spearheaded the civil rights movement of the 1960s. Voting rights was a major goal. It was time the Fifteenth Amendment was honored.[43]

During the 1960s those who took a stand against racism and discrimination knew that their lives were in danger.

In June of 1964, two young civil rights workers named Andrew Goodman and Michael Schwerner went to Philadelphia, Mississippi, to help blacks register to vote. They were met by James Chaney who showed them around. Just outside of town their car was pulled over by a law officer. Two months later their bodies were found in a mud dam in the Tallahaga River. NAACP field secretary Medgar Evers was shot down in front of his house in Mississippi. Viola Liuzzo, a Michigan housewife who had come to take part in the Selma to Montgomery march, was murdered on an Alabama highway.

Although Martin Luther King, Jr., preached nonviolence, his adversaries used every manner of violence to stop his work—from name-calling to imprisonment to physical beatings to murder.

King's message of peace and brotherhood culminated in a speech he gave during the March on Washington in 1963. A. Philip Randolph had helped organize the march, held on the one-hundredth anniversary of the Emancipation Proclamation, for "jobs and freedom." It was the largest-ever demonstration of its kind. Speaking to the two hundred thousand people at the historic march, King spoke of a dream where blacks and whites could live together in harmony. It was a dream not all Americans could envision.

As King had written in "Letter from a Birmingham Jail":

> *We have waited for more than 340 years for our constitutional and God-given rights . . . Perhaps it is easy for those who have never felt the stinging darts of segregation to say, 'Wait!' But when you have seen vicious mobs lynch your mothers and fathers at will and drown your sisters and brothers at whim; when you have seen hate-filled policemen curse, kick and even kill your black brothers and sisters . . . then you will understand why we find it difficult to wait.*[44]

THE MILITANTS

While King talked about peace, brotherhood, and equality, Malcolm X believed the struggle for freedom could only be realized through direct confrontation. He said: "We are fighting for recognition as human beings. We are fighting for the right to live as free humans in this society. In fact, we are actually fighting for rights that are even greater than civil rights and that is human rights. We must have human rights before we can secure civil rights. We must be respected as humans before we can be recognized as citizens."

Born Malcolm Little in May 1925, he changed his name to Malcolm X after becoming a member of the Black Muslims while serving a jail sentence for burglary. Malcolm and others resented the fact that their last names belonged to their former slave masters.[45]

The idea was not a new one. After obtaining their freedom, many blacks had changed their names, or changed the spelling of their names, to distinguish themselves from their former masters' families. In the 1960s there was a reawakening of pride in self and the African heritage. Some blacks chose to rename themselves, selecting an African or Arab name that had special meaning, or simply dropping their last name and using an X. Two well-known examples are boxing champion Cassius Clay, who after becoming a Muslim, changed his name to Muhammad Ali, and basketball great Lou Alcindor, who became Kareem Abdul-Jabbar. New parents gave their babies African names with substance and meaning.

Once he was released from prison, Malcolm X brought a different leadership style and approach to the problem of racism and discrimination. Malcolm rarely used brotherhood and love in his speeches. He talked about "economic rape" and "white oppression." His hard-hitting language and street-wise delivery made him a popular and feared leader.

Today, Malcolm X's speeches don't seem as threatening as they did then. For example, one of the issues he raised in 1963 was economic inequality. Without the resources to produce products or the ability to make decisions in the boardrooms of corporate America, blacks, in his opinion, would always remain second-class citizens. He told youth to think about becoming manufacturers instead of being satisfied with being factory workers. He encouraged blacks to pool their time and talents to compensate for the lack of money.

Both Malcolm X and King were assassinated. On February 21, 1965, at the age of 39, Malcolm X was gunned down at the Audubon Ballroom in New York. Three black men, believed to be angered by Malcolm X's break with Black Muslim leader Elijah Muhammad, were sentenced to life in prison for the crime. All three assassins are free men today. On April 4, 1968, at the age of 39, Martin Luther King, Jr., was killed on the balcony of the Lorraine Motel in Memphis, Tennessee. James Earl Ray was tried and convicted of the murder and is serving a life sentence in Tennessee.

By killing the persons, the assassins believed they could silence their words. They were wrong.[46]

JESSE JACKSON: STANDING ON THE SHOULDERS OF GIANTS

Jesse Jackson was outside the Lorraine Motel when Martin Luther King was killed. In response to King's death, blacks rioted in many cities. Within hours Jackson was back in Chicago trying to calm rioters who were threatening to tear Chicago apart.

While in college at North Carolina A&T, Jesse Jackson had been a leader in the sit-in movement. After his graduation, he went to Chicago, where he attended Chicago Theological Seminary

*Jesse Jackson welcomes Rosa Parks
to the podium before speaking at the
1988 Democratic National Convention.*

and served as the national director of Operation Breadbasket, the economic arm of the Southern Christian Leadership Conference.

After King's death, Jesse Jackson remained loyal to Dr. King's philosophy of peace and brotherhood, while at the same time adopting the outspoken, pride-filled, confrontational style of Malcolm X.

In 1971 he started People United to Save Humanity (PUSH), an organization devoted to combating racism and discrimination within corporate America. The strategy was simple. Operation PUSH documented the hiring practices of a company servicing a largely minority population. If minorities were not fairly represented, a boycott against the company was called. By using this method, PUSH helped to get thousands of minorities and women hired in jobs that had been closed to them prior to the boycott.

Jackson also developed a strong antidrug program directed at America's youth. He used his dynamic speaking ability to motivate students to take responsibility for their actions.

In 1972, New York Congresswoman Shirley Chisolm made an unsuccessful bid for the Democratic Presidential nomination. She was the first African-American to run for the office. It was not until 1984 that Jesse Jackson, another black, made a serious bid for the candidacy. He formed the "Rainbow Coalition" and ran as a candidate of the forgotten groups, those who had no real "say" in government.

He repeated his bid for the Democratic nomination in 1988 and won an even larger number of delegates than in 1984, coming in second to

Michael Dukakis. Jackson's efforts would have been much more difficult had it not been for the work of those who had taken a stand before him. He stood on the shoulders of giants who lifted him up to heights no black man had ever dared reach for.

Jesse Jackson's candidacy demonstrated how far the United States has come with regard to race relations, yet it also showed how much work there is yet to be done before racism and discrimination will be eliminated in America.[47]

SIX

SOME CURRENT ACTIVISTS

Based on the lives of human rights leaders, it is clear there is no single way to take a stand. Each person has to decide whether to take a leadership role or to follow a leader whose beliefs and goals he or she shares. Taking a stand against racism and discrimination is a total commitment. To illustrate the point there is a story about the chicken and the hog.

The chicken and hog were conversing about who gave the most to the farmer. "I give the farmer fresh eggs every day," said the chicken. The hog shook his head. "Fine for you to give an egg," he answered. "For you to give a few eggs is a casual involvement. For me to give bacon is a TOTAL COMMITMENT." Taking a stand against racism and discrimination is not a casual involvement. It is a total commitment.

The following three profiles are about courageous people who challenged acts of racism and discrimination, and against great odds, scored victories.

PORTLAND BIRCHFIELD

In a series of follow-up decisions based on the interpretation of the 1954 *Brown* v. *Board of Education* case, the federal courts ruled that busing would be used to achieve racially balanced schools. The Supreme Court had ordered that all schools integrate "with all deliberate speed." Those who opposed integration had used that clause in the 1954 decision to stall and resist the law. In 1969 the Supreme Court ruled unanimously that school districts all over the country had to end segregation "at once."

The reaction to busing very often has been violent. The National Guard had to be mobilized in Boston to restore order when angry whites rioted over forced busing. They stoned buses carrying black children from one side of town to another. They threw eggs and called out "niggers stay away." The problem was clearly not busing.

The courts have held to their decision. Busing continues. But as we enter the last decade of the twentieth century, statistics show that American schools are far from racially balanced. Many districts are still under court order to come up with voluntary desegregation programs or be prepared to obey court-appointed administration of their district.

Many blacks and whites who are not necessarily racists don't like the idea of busing or court orders. Neighborhood schools are preferable, but most neighborhoods are not racially balanced. Therein lies the problem.

Parkway South is a large high school located in a midwestern suburb. Except for a few black families who live in the area, the school district serves a mostly white, upper-middle-class community.

In the mid-1980s, court-ordered busing, coupled with a volunteer desegregation program, increased the minority school population from less than 1 percent to 15 percent. Most of the black students are bused to Parkway from the inner city. Portland Birchfield began freshman year at Parkway after having attended predominately black inner-city schools all her life.

"White teachers and students had all kinds of stereotypical ideas about city kids. I guess they get their ideas off television," reflects a poised nineteen-year-old Portland Birchfield. "Some kids thought we were cutthroats, druggie rapists. And I guess we black kids had our stereotypes, too. Some who were willing to take the time learned that the stereotypes were wrong. That's what the busing program is about, trying to put black kids and white kids together so they don't grow up so ignorant about each other."[48]

Portland's district is typical of the problem that exists all over the country. The suburbs are mostly white and the inner city is mostly black and other *poor* minorities. In order for children of different races and social and economic backgrounds to learn to live together in harmony, something has to be done about the way they are educated. Busing is not the best answer. Nobody will argue that. What will take its place?

When Portland Birchfield entered Parkway South in her freshman year she was admittedly frightened. "Being a freshman is bad enough, but it's twice as bad when you're in a new environment and a definite minority. It was like culture shock for me," remembers Portland. "There was plenty of racism, but nobody wanted to admit it. It was like, push it under the rug and pretend that it doesn't exist, and it will magically go away."

During Portland's first two years in high school she observed the effects of racism on her friends and herself. "I kept a notebook and I just wrote down my impressions about what I saw." She noted that some black students tried to find acceptance by discarding everything that was associated with their culture. "I knew that wasn't for me. But being so black that I couldn't relate to anything or anybody wasn't an answer either."

She also observed whites and how they related to nonwhite students. "Some were genuinely okay," she says. "They were usually people who could relate to others without a lot of hang-ups."

Portland believes that racism is the result of poor self-image. "Racists are, in my opinion, those who are trying to find someone to feel superior over because they don't feel good about themselves."

One day in class a boy called Portland a nigger. "I wanted to smack him, but I didn't," she says shaking her head to dismiss the feelings that obviously still accompany the hurt of the incident. "I didn't know what to do. Fighting would only add to the problem. Something had to be done with my anger and something needed to be done about the situation—things needed to be brought out into the open. So I started writing."

Portland wrote poetry and stories. Then in her senior year she took a drama class from Mrs. Phyllis Abling. "When Portland showed me her writings, I saw a lot of potential in her material," says Mrs.

Abling. That's when Portland asked about writing and producing an original play that would tackle the tough issues of racism and discrimination as they existed at Parkway South.

At first, Mrs. Abling suggested that the class produce a play that had already been written. But Portland insisted that an original play would be more effective, because it would be tailored to the specific incidents at Parkway. Portland argued that the play would be more meaningful to the audience if they could identify with the characters, setting, and dialogue. Mrs. Abling agreed to look at Portland's play once it was written to decide if it was of presentation quality.

"I wasn't surprised that she wrote it and that it was good," says Mrs. Abling. "Portland was—and still is—a determined, confident, and mature young woman."

Portland's play, *All About People*, went into production. Portland was selected as the director. "Casting, set design, rehearsals . . . everything that has to be done to get a play produced was my responsibility," she says, "and it is not easy."

Dwight Collins, an actor who has had parts in the film *The Color Purple* and some television productions, visited Parkway. He learned about Portland's play and promised to return and give her some pointers on directing. "His help was invaluable," remembers Portland. "It was like a dream come true working with a real professional."

The play, which dealt with all kinds of racial stereotyping among both teachers and students, was met with mixed reviews. "All the school saw it, and it was featured one evening for parents and community. Some of the faculty were outraged. A few parents complained, too, about the play being one-sided. But a large majority of the audiences saw what I was trying to do and enjoyed it."

Portland believes that some people were uncomfortable with the play's topic because they recognized themselves in some of the characters. Although Portland insists that most of the characters were composites, she did admit that some of the incidents were from actual accounts.

The production achieved what Portland wanted. "It got people to talking about some of the problems in our school, in our community, in our country. I think some people even learned from it." What more could a playwright ask?

Portland graduated in June 1988 and plans to attend college and major in drama. "At first I didn't think writing a play could make a difference to anyone but me. But, I found out that a play, a book, a poem, all kinds of creative expression can be a powerful way of making a statement. I'm going to do it again for sure."

GEORGE SAKAGUCHI

George Sakaguchi was seventeen years old on December 7, 1941. He and his father Tomokichi listened to the reports of the Japanese attack on Pearl Harbor with the same surprise and fear that all Americans did. Living at the time in a farm community outside Fresno, California, the Sakaguchis were, like many of their neighbors, poor tenant farmers who scratched out a living working in the fields. "We had no political clout, no special interests in Sacramento or Washington," says Mr. Sakaguchi.[49]

"My father came to America in the early 1920s," he recalls. "But at the time, he couldn't become an American citizen." Although there was a wave of European immigration between 1900 and 1925, Asian immigration was curtailed by a series of restrictive laws. According to the journal *Redress* produced by the Japanese American Citizens League (JACL), in 1909 Asians were "discriminated against, forced to live in segregated areas, denied public accommodations, and in general, faced constant attacks from newspapers, politicians, and organizations." In 1913, California passed the Alien Land Law, which prevented Asians from owning land, and in 1920 a stricter law was passed that denied Japanese immigrants citizenship. By 1924, the Oriental Exclusions Act halted all immigration from Far East nations.

"The first generation of immigrants were called *issei*, meaning "the first." The second generation, called *nisei*, were citizens. Children born of Japanese immigrants were naturalized citizens," Mr. Sakaguchi explained. "I am a nisei . . . born American."

Racism and discrimination against all Asians—Chinese, Japanese and Filipinos—was rampant on the West Coast. Nisei children worked hard at overcoming racism by becoming exemplary citizens. "The general feeling was if we caused no trouble, then no trouble would come to us." But Mr. Sakaguchi and many of his fellow Americans of Japanese ancestry were wrong in making that assumption.

After Pearl Harbor, the exclusion of the ethnic Japanese from the West Coast was recommended to Secretary of War Henry L. Stimson by Lt. General John L. DeWitt, commanding general of the Western Defense Command with responsibility for West Coast security. He wrote to the president:

> *The Japanese race is an enemy race and while many second and third generation Japanese born on United States soil, possessed of United States citizenship, have become 'Americanized,' the racial strains are undiluted . . . It, therefore, follows that along the vital Pacific Coast over 112,000 potential enemies of Japanese extraction, are at large today.*[50]

Although the FBI and Navy assured government officials that DeWitt was overreacting, and that there was no sabotage committed in Hawaii or on the mainland, nobody seemed to hear. Outlandish statements were made by Congressmen Tom Stewart of Tennessee and John Rankin of Mississippi. According to Stewart, "No Japanese should have the right to claim American citizenship," and Rankin ranted that "This is a race war . . . I say it is of vital importance that we get rid of every Japanese . . . Let us get rid of them now!"[50]

On February 19, 1942, ten weeks after Pearl Harbor, President Franklin Delano Roosevelt signed Executive Order No. 9066 which resulted in the removal of all Japanese-Americans—those called "aliens" and their native-born children. Here is a listing of the ten major detention camps:

1. Amache, Colorado (7,318 persons)
2. Gila River, Arizona (13,348 persons)
3. Heart Mountain, Wyoming (10,767 persons)

4. Jerome, Arkansas (8,497 persons)
5. Manzanar,California (10,046 persons)
6. Minidoka, Idaho (9,397 persons)
7. Rohwer, Arkansas (8,475 persons)
8. Tule Lake, California (18,789 persons)
9. Topaz, Utah (8,130 persons)
10. Poston, Arizona (17,814 persons)

"My mother had died several years earlier," remembers George Sakaguchi, who was a junior in high school in 1942. "And my two older sisters had moved back to Japan to live with an uncle. My youngest sister was being raised by a white family, so there was just my father and me. I remember clearly, we were taken first to an assembly center where we stayed until November 1942. Then we were shipped to Arkansas."

The cheaply built tar-paper housing was quickly constructed. Although there was no widespread physical cruelty inflicted upon the internees, the internment camp was a drab, mentally abusive place. "It was so nonproductive. I remember that I kept asking myself what had we done to deserve this? The answer kept coming up *nothing!* We were victims, feeling very guilty about something we didn't know what or why for."

For the most part, the Japanese-Americans were stunned by the government's action against them. Clearly their constitutional rights were being violated. "One of the myths about the internment was that Japanese-Americans didn't try to defend themselves and that they were passive. That is not true. There are three cases that challenged the legality of the internment at the time," says Mr. Sakaguchi. "None of them were favorable to us however. At the time, I wasn't aware of all the legal battles that were being waged. All I knew was that we were behind wire fences, and nobody was giving explanations. Our parents told us to behave, be quiet, and do what we were told. Challenging the federal government was out of the question. But I had plenty of questions. At seventeen, eighteen, I was full of them! But we didn't talk about it much."

At the end of 1942, the military came to the camps and asked for volunteers among the nisei. Each volunteer had to pass a loyalty review. Many young men volunteered for the army, hoping to prove by their example that their parents were innocent of any wrongdoing toward the United States. Not long afterwards some of the nisei were drafted, but a few chose to go to prison, arguing that they would not go into combat until their families' liberties were restored.

Young men taken from the ten internment camps formed the 442nd Regiment Combat Team. The 100th Battalion was raised in Hawaii, and it was with this unit that Senator Daniel Inouye lost his arm in combat in Italy. The Japanese-American fighting units were the most decorated in the war. For young men like George Sakaguchi, the Japanese-American soldier was a hero.

"The story of Frank Hachiya is a war hero story I recall . . . one that is both well known and typical of what Japanese-Americans had to endure," says Mr. Sakaguchi.

On December 30, 1944, Sgt. Hachiya parachuted behind enemy lines in the Philippines. His mission was to scout Japanese defense positions, which he did. But on the way back to the American lines, he was mistaken for a Japanese soldier and shot by American fire. Though wounded, he did not stop until he completed his mission, delivering the maps to his commanding officer. He died three days later of his wounds.

Meanwhile in Sgt. Hachiya's hometown of Hood River, Oregon, the American Legion had voted to remove the names of fourteen Japanese-Americans, including Hachiya's, from the honor roll. When Sgt. Hachiya was awarded the Distinguished Service Cross posthumously, the fourteen names were reinstated.

"I was released from the Arkansas camp in February 1943," George Sakaguchi continues. Following the examples of his wartime heroes, George Sakaguchi joined the army in February of 1945 and served until 1951, after which he attended Washington University in St. Louis and worked as a civilian in the Defense Department's Mapping Division.

For many years, what happened to Japanese-Americans during World War II was not discussed. But very few who experienced the situation ever forgot it. During the 1964 annual convention of the JACL, the Redress Committee was formed. George Sakaguchi was a member. "I felt at the time that it was one of the most important things I would ever do in my life. And it was."

As a result of the Redress Committee's work, Congress passed an act creating a Commission on Wartime Relocation and Internment of Civilians. Three years later, in 1983, the commission issued a report, stating "military necessity did not exist in fact to justify the evacuation and exclusion of ethnic Japanese from the West Coast . . . and exclusion was the result of 'race prejudice, war hysteria, and a failure of political leadership.' " Estimated monetary loss to ethnic Japanese was between $2 to $6 billion dollars, for which the JACL asked for personal redress along with a national apology.[53]

In August 1988 President Ronald Reagan signed a resolution passed by Congress, recognizing that a grave injustice was done to Japanese-Americans and their parents and offering the apologies of the nation for the acts of exclusion, removal, and detention. In addition, a payment of $20,000 was to be paid to each of the approximately 60,000 surviving internees.

George Sakaguchi describes how he felt watching President Reagan sign the resolution. "The apology meant more to me than the money. America had said *I am sorry,* and it felt good through and through. The victims were finally exonerated."

Although the redress resolution had passed, the work of Mr. Sakaguchi was not over. He served as a national chairman of the Awards Committee of the JACL, and he is presently serving on the committee to restore an internment camp at Rohwer, Arkansas. "There is a cemetery holding the remains of those who died in the camps. We must not forget them or why they were there." Efforts are being made to make the camp a historical site, and the local residents are in full support of it.

George Sakaguchi summarizes his teenage experience in strongly felt words. "The pain and hurt never really goes away. I was seventeen when my world came crashing in on me. It took many years for the hurt to pass, but what makes me feel good is that the story is finally out in the open. We stood up! I stood up, and we won!"

MRS. BEULAH MAE DONALD

Nineteen-year-old Michael Donald hoped to be a brick mason. He had a part-time job at *The Press Register* newspaper in Mobile, Alabama, to help finance his study at a trade school.

On the night of March 21, 1981, two Ku Klux Klansmen, Henry Hays and James ("Tiger") Knowles, selected Michael to be "an example." It is believed the two Klansmen were angry about a mistrial involving a black man accused of killing a white police officer. After cruising through the black community, Hays and Knowles spotted Michael walking alone. Police reports show that he had left his sister's house about 11:00 P.M. Stopping and pretending to need directions, the Klansmen lured their unsuspecting victim to the car and forced him inside at gunpoint. Michael's horribly beaten body was found hanging from a tree the next morning.[54]

Michael's mother, Mrs. Beulah Mae Donald, knew her son's death was a meaningless murder. She had seen the work of the Klan before, having been born in De Lisle, Mississippi, where Klan activities were not uncommon. There have been numerous unsolved murders believed to have been committed by Klansmen against blacks, Jews, Catholics, and others. But everybody wondered if a Klan killing would go unpunished in 1981. Mrs. Beulah Mae Donald decided to stand up to the Klan for her dead son. "He was a good child," she told an *Ebony* magazine reporter. "I wanted to get to the bottom of just what happened," she says, "so his living would not have been in vain."

According to Alabama State Senator Michael

Figures, who is black, Mrs. Donald is "the typical black matriarch who has struggled to keep her family together." The divorced mother of six children is now a grandmother who finds time to volunteer for the foster grandparents program when her health permits. Mrs. Donald is a quiet, gentle person whose faith is the cornerstone of her strength.

Right after Michael's death, it was speculated that he might have been involved in drugs or some other crime. It appeared at first that the case would end up "unsolved" like so many similar cases had in the past. Dissatisfied with the way the case was handled, family members, led by Michael's sister, picketed the courthouse. The protest mushroomed and 10,000 people, including Jesse Jackson, rallied to call for justice.

The protest brought the case to national attention, but it was no closer to being solved than it had been before. Many doubted that it ever would be solved. Going against the "Invisible Empire" was not an easy task.

But the South was a different place than it had been twenty or thirty years before. When an FBI investigation turned up nothing, Assistant U.S. Attorney Thomas Figures (the state senator's brother) urged the Justice Department to conduct another investigation, and this time it led to the arrest of Knowles and Hays.

After three years, Mrs. Donald finally knew who had killed her son and why. Tiger Knowles testified against the Klan, telling how he and Hays had brutally murdered a person for no other reason than that they wanted to kill somebody black— it didn't matter as long as he or she was black.

place. Tar-and-featherings were a Saturday-evening picnic. During the 1920s membership into the Klan increased. After World War II membership declined but was revitalized again by Samuel Green.

By using fear and violence, the Klan resisted every move toward freedom, justice, and equality of the races. And they succeeded. Nothing was more frightening than a burning cross in the front yard of a person's home. No black ever challenged the Klan without some terrible retaliation.

At first sight Mrs. Donald does not seem a likely challenger of the notorious Klan. But with the help of Senator Michael Figures, Mrs. Donald made her decision. "I wasn't afraid of Klan retaliation," she says. "They had done all it was that could be done to a mother . . . kill one of her children. What more could they do? So, I said 'Let's do it.' "

She filed suit and in February 1987 an all-white jury in Mobile, Alabama brought in a verdict that the Klan was liable for the criminal acts of its members. The court awarded Mrs. Donald a $7 million settlement against the United Klans of America and six of its members. She was given the deed to the Klan's national headquarters near Tuscaloosa, Alabama. It was sold and the money awarded to Mrs. Donald.

"I wasn't concerned about the money. I wanted justice," says Mrs. Donald. Her landmark victory

A Ku Klux Klan
cross-burning in 1986.

also sent a clear message to the Klan and other racist organizations that they are not above the law. Her story proves that when people take a stand against racism, they *can* make a difference.[55]

SEVEN

STRENGTH IN NUMBERS

One person crying out against injustice can make a dramatic statement. But when people organize, their collective voice is very powerful. There is strength in numbers. Joining or supporting an organization that represents your beliefs is a way to become involved. If you are interested in working with others, discuss your interests with your parents and teachers. Ask them to help you choose an organization that shares your point of view. Here are just a few organizations dedicated to fighting racism and discrimination.

NATIONAL ASSOCIATION FOR THE ADVANCEMENT OF COLORED PEOPLE (NAACP)

The NAACP is one of the oldest and largest civil rights organizations in America, with over 2,000 branches in all fifty states, including military bases in Hawaii, Japan, and Germany. Membership totals 400,000 and includes people of all races. The national executive director is Benjamin Hooks. Annual membership for children up to age 18 is $3. For adults the annual dues are $10.

Roy Wilkins, a former national executive director of the NAACP, clearly outlined the procedure for taking a stand against racism and discrimination at the historic 1963 March on Washington: "When we return home, keep up the speaking by letters and telegrams and telephone and whenever possible, by personal visits."

According to Dr. Esther Nelson, a member of the Sacramento NAACP branch office, "our purpose today is to keep people aware of the real issues. The struggle [for equality] is not over."

One of the most exciting programs sponsored by the NAACP is the Academic, Cultural, Technical, Scientific Olympics program (ACTSO). Students are encouraged to submit projects, essays, poems, photography—all kinds of projects—which are judged first on the local level, then sent to compete on a national level. Scholarships are granted to the winners.

In addition to local programs, the NAACP is instrumental in helping to watchdog political appointments, legislation, Supreme Court and lower court appointments and decisions, anything that is in the interest of minorities. The NAACP serves as a sounding board for minority concerns. Its *Crisis* magazine keeps members informed.

For example, one major concern of the NAACP is judgeships, and especially Supreme Court justices. History has shown how justices have interpreted the Constitution differently: compare *Plessy* v. *Ferguson,* which upheld segregation, with *Brown* v. *Board of Education,* which ended segregation. Because of the important role that justices play in the interpretation of the Constitution, the

NAACP has led the fight against the appointment of several Supreme Court justices.

G. Harrold Carswell of Florida was nominated as a justice by President Richard Nixon. The NAACP, after studying Carswell's civil rights record as a lower court judge, opposed his confirmation. Carswell had made the comment that "Segregation of the races is proper and the only practical and correct way of life in our states." He also participated in a campaign to exclude blacks from a Tallahassee golf club, and reportedly insulted civil rights lawyers in court. The NAACP, along with other groups, rallied successfully to defeat his confirmation.[56]

In 1987, President Ronald Reagan nominated Robert Bork to be a Supreme Court Justice. While Bork was, without a doubt, intellectually brilliant, many people were concerned about his ultra-conservative opinions regarding the Constitution, and his positions on civil rights. During Bork's confirmation hearings, it was disclosed that he had left a "paper trail" of writings from which his opponents could quote. He could not deny his comments. Legal analysts have stated that Bork's own words helped to defeat him.

In retrospect, the question remains: Would Robert Bork have been swayed any more or less than any other justice by his political ideology? His supporters say no, but his opponents, led by Massachusetts Senator Edward M. Kennedy and the NAACP, believed that his record suggested that he would. The NAACP rallied their forces and asked their half-million members to send a clear message to their representatives regarding the Bork confirmation. It resulted in one of the largest letter-writing campaigns in the organization's history.

Andrew Kopkind, a political analyst, stated: "One after another Southern Democrats who wouldn't have dreamed of supporting Northern liberals in a straight ideological struggle 10 to 20 years ago, joined in the vote against Bork." Blacks and other minorities are voters. When they sent a message through their organizations, the politicians listened and voted accordingly.[57]

THE URBAN LEAGUE

In 1918 a group of New York social workers began the National Urban League. Their purpose was to help rural blacks, migrating from the South to the North, to adjust to urban living. Assistance included help in finding housing, job training, education, and employment.

Today the Urban League has 112 affiliates from coast to coast. John E. Jacob is the President and Chief Executive Officer. National headquarters are located in New York. Membership is $5 per year for students up to age 18. Membership entitles youth members to participate in summer job programs designed to help students build self-esteem, gain confidence, and improve work skills.

The National Urban League also holds an annual essay contest, open to high school seniors and college students. Winners are awarded $1,000 scholarships. For 1989 the essay theme was "How do you think education should change to help people from different cultures to understand each other and live together peacefully?"

"Each Urban League office serves the needs of the community," says Beth Williams, executive assistant to Mr. George Dean, director of the Sacramento, California office. "We push for academic excellence." Mrs. Williams proudly explained how the four-year-old Early Start Program (ESP) was a model of how community, school, and family could work together to offset the negative influence of inner-city living. Gang participation, drug sale and use, teenage pregnancy, low academic achievement, and crime are the major causes of the high drop-out rate of minority children, especially Hispanics and blacks. "So far," says Mrs. Williams, "our program has a 97 percent success rate. Our participants are staying in school, doing well, and feeling good about it."

The ESP program in Sacramento is not unlike many other programs that are functioning in communities all over the country. "The problem," says Mrs. Williams, "is that we don't have enough of them."

At the 1964 National Urban League convention, former executive director Whitney Young helped set the focus of the organization for the last decades of the twentieth century. He said: "Our citizens must also march beyond protest to *participation*. We must march to PTA meetings, to libraries, to voting booths. We must march to . . . adult education classes, to vocational and apprentice training courses . . . We must march to decision-making meetings on town zoning, urban renewal, health, welfare, and education. These are the sensitive points."[58]

B'NAI B'RITH

B'nai B'rith (meaning "sons of the covenant") is the oldest Jewish organization in the United States, founded in 1843. Today it has close to half a million members. Auxiliary groups include the Hillel

Foundation, generally located on college campuses, designed to form a link between Jewish students and their culture, and the Anti-Defamation League.

The Anti-Defamation League was founded in 1913 to combat anti-Semitism after a Georgia mob lynched a Jew accused of killing a young factory worker. Although he was innocent, the mob, aroused by Ku Klux Klan propaganda, dragged the man from his cell and hanged him.

Like the NAACP, the organization has fought against racism and discrimination, not just against Jews, but in support of all victims of bigotry. One of the strongest supporters of the civil rights movement in the 1960s was B'nai B'rith.

B'nai B'rith and the Anti-Defamation League sponsor local seminars, lecture series, and symposiums. Members and their families are kept informed of organization activities and concerns through newsletters, reading lists, and after-school meetings.

There are local chapters of B'nai B'rith throughout the United States, Canada, and Europe. Membership is open to all those over age 18, and dues vary from chapter to chapter.[59]

THE AMERICAN CIVIL LIBERTIES UNION (ACLU)

The American Civil Liberties Union (ACLU) was founded in 1920 to defend, without charge, the rights of men and women "set forth in the Declaration of Independence and the Constitution." The ACLU will legally defend any person regardless of race, sex, creed, religious or nonreligious affiliation, or political persuasion if that person's rights, as guaranteed by the Constitution, have been denied. Today, practically all the ACLU's cases are based on the first ten amendments.

Long before it was popular to do so, the ACLU defended blacks in civil rights cases. When the organization spoke out against the Japanese internment during World War II, calling it "the worst single wholesale violation of civil rights of American citizens in our history," it was criticized for "siding with the enemy."

But criticism is not something the ACLU avoids. Many of the cases they choose to represent are controversial, but none more so than the Skokie Nazi march case in the 1970s.

A neo-Nazi group wanted to conduct a march in Skokie, Illinois, a town with a large Jewish population, including many concentration camp survivors. The Anti-Defamation League of B'nai B'rith argued that the Nazi group chose Skokie just to harass the community and therefore, to avoid trouble, the Nazis should not be permitted to march.

The ACLU countered that the Nazi group was covered by the *same* rights that had allowed civil rights workers to hold marches in the segregated South. White citizens had claimed in the 1960s that black civil rights marchers were troublemakers, too. If the Nazis were denied their rights, then the rights of all Americans were in jeopardy. The reason the Constitution works so well is that it does not limit the rights of people based on whether their ideas are acceptable to a majority of the people, or popular at the time. The Nazi message is hateful and mean, but that is not the issue. The ACLU defended the Nazis' First Amendment right of free speech and assembly. In order for justice to be fair, it must truly be blind.

The ACLU has also handled a number of cases regarding student issues and student rights, such as the search of student lockers, using dogs in schools to sniff students for drugs, and school library book censorship, to name a few.

The national headquarters of the ACLU is in New York; however, each state has an autonomous affiliate which can choose its own cases, raise money, and hold membership drives independent of the other states. Volunteer lawyers and support staff handle the cases, but each ACLU affiliate pays the court costs, which can be very expensive. The $20 membership fee entitles the member to *Civil Liberties*, the national newsletter. Students are welcomed by most affiliates and the student membership is $5. According to Joyce Armstrong, Executive Director of the Eastern Missouri office, "Our student members help with fundraising activities. It gives them an opportunity to meet other people and get involved."

PEOPLE UNITED TO SAVE HUMANITY (OPERATION PUSH)

Rev. Jesse Jackson started People United to Save Humanity (PUSH), headquartered in Chicago, Illinois, in 1972. Jackson's energy and personal commitment made the organization what it is. For example, he established four organizational goals: voter registration, economic development among blacks and other minorities, education of youth, and international development.

In 1984 Jackson pointed out that eighty-five million people—or 47 percent of eligible voters—did not vote in the presidential election, and fifty-four million of these people were not registered. An all-out voter registration campaign launched by PUSH and the Rainbow Coalition (Jackson's political organization) registered thousands of new voters. Their votes helped Jackson make a second serious bid for the presidency in 1988.

PUSH has an educational program called PUSH/EXCEL that uses parents, athletes, disk jockeys, ministers, and entertainers to encourage minority youths to stay in school and achieve. Long before it became a national issue, Jesse Jackson used the PUSH/EXCEL program to teach thousands of students about the dangers of drug abuse. He still speaks candidly about drug use, gangs, teen pregnancy, and other problems facing young people all over the country in urban, suburban, and rural schools. The hallmark of Jesse Jackson's delivery is his call: "Repeat after me: I am somebody!" This confirmation of one's own self-worth is, in Jackson's opinion, the foundation upon which learning can be built. PUSH/EXCEL is always in need of volunteers to help with their various educational programs.

The economic boycott is a tool PUSH has used very effectively. If a company or business fails to comply with affirmative action for minorities—including women—or use black-produced goods and services, PUSH calls for a strike against the company until concessions are made. Under Jackson's leadership PUSH has taken on major food chains, department stores, beverage companies, and banks. "Power," he explains, "is the ability to achieve purpose."

The purpose of PUSH (and the Rainbow Coalition) is to use direct action, litigation, consumer boycotts, and various forms of moral persuasion to gain "equity and parity (our share) of the great American pie."[61]

THE MARTIN LUTHER KING CENTER FOR NONVIOLENT SOCIAL CHANGE

After the assassination of Martin Luther King in 1968, his wife, Coretta Scott King, helped start the King Center for Nonviolent Social Change in Atlanta, Georgia. In 1970 she told *Ebony* reporter Charles L. Sanders, "I'm committed to the development of it, to raising funds for it. There *must* be a proper memorial to Martin and all those who died in the nonviolent struggle. There *must* be a monument to the man and the movement which changed the course of history for black people and deprived people in the United States; which forced more change in 13 years than had been achieved in an entire century. I'm not talking about erecting a statue or something like that. We're going to build a living memorial—a place where there is activity and *life*." In 1988, her son Dexter King became president of the center but Mrs. King is still active and helps set many of the center's policies.

The King Center has a full-time staff that helps operate the King memorial, although they still depend largely upon volunteer help. There is a museum, a bookstore, and a library. Classes in nonviolent protests and demonstrations are held regularly. Millions of people from all over the world have visited the center since 1970, and busloads of tourists come daily. School children, senior citizens, and all those in between come to learn the techniques of nonviolent protest. Recently the center selected a group of teachers from all over the country to design a curriculum for teaching nonviolent activism.

Through Mrs. King's efforts and the support of millions of people, Dr. Martin Luther King's birthday, January 15th, is now a national holiday, an honor never before bestowed on a black person in the United States. The King Center welcomes letters regarding issues that affect civil rights in America. According to a volunteer, thousands of birthday cards are received each January wishing Dr. King a happy birthday. "It's like they think of him as still living, and as long as a person is remembered then they are still alive."[62]

RELIGION AGAINST RACISM

In *Great Negroes Past and Present* Russell Adams states: "The African Methodist Episcopal Church has the distinction of being the oldest and largest institution among black Americans." The AME Church was founded in 1787, when Richard Allen, a former slave, refused to worship in segregated seating at St. George's Church in Philadelphia. Allen represented the black members in a formal complaint to the pastor, who responded that Allen could either worship in segregated facilities and in silence or not at all.

Allen chose neither of those options. He left St. George's and started Bethel African Methodist Episcopal Church, the first black church in America. Between 1815 and 1830 Richard Allen was the commonly recognized leader of free blacks in the North. He was a spiritual and political leader as well. His Bethel Church was the scene of many political meetings and a center for abolitionists.

Black clergymen have been, since slavery times, both political and spiritual leaders. In *Roll, Jordan, Roll: The World the Slaves Made,* Eugene D. Genovese writes, "The black preacher faced a problem analogous to that of the early Christian preachers. They had to speak a language defiant enough to hold the high-spirited among their flock, but neither so inflammatory as to rouse them to battles they could not win nor so ominous as to rouse the ire of ruling powers."[65]

Like Allen, other black clergymen have taken leadership roles in the struggle for civil and human rights all over the world. Rev. Dr. Martin Luther King, Jr., and Rev. Ralph Abernathy, leaders of the Southern Christian Leadership Conference (SCLC) were both ordained ministers. Andrew Young, a former SCLC aide and currently the mayor of Atlanta, Georgia, is an ordained minister, and so is Rev. Jesse Jackson.

Bishop Desmond Tutu, the 1984 Nobel Peace Prize winner, was named the Anglican Bishop of Johannesburg in November 1984. In the tradition of Martin Luther King, Bishop Tutu is a political activist as well as a clergyman. In South Africa, where Bishop Tutu lives and serves, 70 percent of the people are black, yet the government is controlled solely by whites. Black South Africans are not permitted to vote in national elections. They can only live or own land in certain areas. Black children cannot receive the same education as whites. People can be held in prison without being charged with a crime. Bishop Tutu is trying to bring about change through nonviolent protests. He has asked that all democratic nations stop trading with South Africa to protest their system of apartheid.

Two major denominations have chosen black women as their spiritual leaders. Rev. Joan Salmon Campbell of West Chester, Pennsylvania, was elected moderator of the Presbyterian Church in June 1989. Affectionately known as "Rev. Joan," she will preside over the general assembly and represent the denomination to the rest of the world. She is the first black clergywoman to lead the three-million-member denomination.

In early 1989, Barbara Harris became associate bishop of the Episcopal Church in Massachusetts. "I'm proud of my sister and I'm proud to stand with her," says Rev. Joan. "We are both leaders in our churches, particularly at a time when our denominations are under such fire and criticism."

While the Catholic Church is opposed to women's ordination, it took a firm stand against racism and discrimination. Pope John Paul II asked the Pontifical Commission "Iustitia et Pax" to "help enlighten and awaken consciences about racial prejudice and discrimination." In 1988, the commission issued its report, entitled "The Church and Racism: Towards a More Fraternal Society."[66]

The forty-three-page document details the history and the various forms of racism. The commission clearly stated the Catholic Church's position on racial prejudice, saying:

> *Racial Prejudice, which denies the equal dignity of all the members of the human family and blasphemes the Creator, can only be eradicated by going to its roots, where it is formed: in the human heart. It is from the heart that just and unjust behavior is born, according to whether persons are open to God's will—in the natural order and in the Living Word—or whether they close themselves up in those egoisms dictated by fear or the instinct of domination. It is the way we look at others that must be purified. Harboring racist thoughts and entertaining racist attitudes is a sin against the specific message of Christ for whom one's "neighbor" is not only a person from my tribe, my milieu, my religion, or my nation: it is every person that I meet along the way.*

The commission suggested the following goals to their worldwide congregations with the purpose of helping to diminish the impact of racism and discrimination:

1. to appeal to a change of heart
2. to form convictions and consciences through well-represented Christian doctrine and witness
3. to defend the victims of racism
4. to intervene in an evangelical and positive way even against those who abet racism
5. to make use of schools and education to instill respect for others

6. to work to improve the texts of laws and institutions[67]

Similarly, the Lutheran Church–Missouri Synod passed a resolution at their 1986 National Convention that makes a strong statement against racism and discrimination. Political, social, and religious organizations are taking a stand against racism and discrimination all over the world. Wherever you live, work, worship, and learn there is a way to become involved.

EIGHT

ACT!
DON'T REACT!

Racism is an emotionally charged subject. If you've ever been discriminated against, you know it is difficult to think rationally or act calmly. The first reaction is to attack or retreat. But it is imperative, when taking a stand against racism or discrimination, that you state your case directly, fairly, and accurately, using facts—documented evidence—to support your claims. Anything less will be ineffective and may, in some cases, be counterproductive.

Wild accusations, rumor, hearsay, and verbal attacks only serve to undermine your credibility and forfeit the legitimacy of your case. Remember the boy who cried wolf too often? Be careful not to use racism and discrimination as a crutch. For example, being kept after school is not necessarily a racist act on the part of your teacher. Your not making the basketball team does not make the coach a bigot. Before accusing a person of a very serious offense, take an honest look at your behavior and at your ability and determine if the accusations are valid. If, however, you believe you do have grounds, log your complaints with school authorities.

Becoming an activist doesn't necessarily mean your position is right or that your stand will bring about any measurable change. More often than not, activists have unpopular opinions considered too radical for "mainstream" thinking. Historically, students have been in the forefront of social change. In America, turn-of-the-century college women were leaders in the women's suffrage movement. North Carolina A & T students in Greensboro held sit-ins at Woolworth's in the winter of 1960, which served as a model for other students in other cities across the nation. Students led protests against South African apartheid in the 1980s, just as they organized the anti-Vietnam War protests of the 1970s.

Simply getting angry doesn't change a thing. Avoiding confrontation only allows the situation to get worse. An individual act of courage can make the difference between a peaceful settlement and better understanding as opposed to mistrust and violence. In 1956, following a school desegregation order, twelve black students tried to register at the previously all-white high school in Clinton, Tennessee. A white supremacist stirred up the population to the rioting point. Hostilities were running high among the 4,000 residents. But fifty white students, led by the seventeen-year-old football captain, calmly asked the community to comply with the federal court order. He reminded them of their responsibility to obey the law. The adults, shamed by their own irrational behavior, supported their children, and Clinton schools were desegregated without further incident.[68]

College students blockading a hall to protest university investments in companies that do business with South Africa.

BECOMING AN ACTIVIST

An activist is a person who gets involved in order to bring about changes. Jesse Jackson defines himself as an activist:

> *I am not a political purist; I'm a political activist. I make political decisions. I choose to vote in an imperfect political system because I'm a political activist. I deal with Democrats, Republicans, non-aligned, unregistered, and disinterested because I am an activist. I am involved in the affairs of my day. I am not a referee, not an arm-chair philosopher, not a grandstand spectator. I believe in activity.*[69]

Activity is the key word—involvement, participation. Let your anger, fear, even your disgust, lead you to positive action, responsible confrontation. Here are a few suggestions for taking an active part in helping to decrease racism and discrimination in your school and community. (Seek help and advice from parents, teachers, counselors, or priest, rabbi or pastor.)

• Keep a journal; write about your feelings, your fears and frustrations about race. Directing your emotions through creative channels helps produce excellent poems and stories. Perhaps you would prefer to sketch your feelings or express them musically.

• Talk to your parents about your feelings. Plan family activities that enhance your knowledge of different races.

• Become a pen pal with a person of another race.

• Read a biography of a famous member of a minority. Share the book with family or friends. Perhaps start a history reading group. Maybe start a multicultural social club.

• Write or produce a classroom play that handles the subject of racism and discrimination in an instructive way.

• Write an article for the school newspaper, then perhaps a letter to the editor of your local newspaper or a national magazine.

• Attend a multicultural activity with family or friends.

• Organize a letter-writing campaign to your local, state, or federal officials regarding a discrimination issue, such as red-lining (refusal to serve a minority area) by a particular insurance company or bank, housing discrimination practices by a particular realty company, etc.

• Organize a boycott of a company or product that is guilty of discrimination.

• Take an active part in planning next year's black history month celebration and/or the Martin Luther King Birthday celebration in your school, church, or community.

• Take a person of another race to your church.

• Work for a political candidate whose positions are clear regarding racism and discrimination.

A public service ad sponsored by General Dynamics gave some startling statistics: "In the last Presidential election, only 53% of those eligible actually voted. The problem is worse among the youngest voters, the 18-to-24-year-old group. Less than half

of them even register. Only 17% actually voted in 1986." The ad warns that "when a government is of half the people and by half the people, sooner or later the worst thing happens. It becomes for half the people. And no American would vote for that."[70]

Another responsible and effective way to take a stand on racism and discrimination is to know your own position and then know the people who represent you. Even before you can vote, it is important to know your local school board official, councilperson, district attorney, state senator, congressman, mayor, governor. What do their records reflect? Listen beyond the rhetoric and high-sounding words. Remember, a speechwriter writes most political speeches; the politician delivers them. Get beyond the media image and their "stage presence." Hear what is not being said as well as what is being said. Be informed so that when you can vote you can vote intelligently.

Elected officials come and go, but the legacy they leave behind will be affecting the course of American life two hundred years later. Today our nation stands for equality, justice, and freedom

*Read and study
all you can about
the issues that
concern you.
Command of facts
and opinions will
help you win over
your opponents.*

based on constitutional guarantees. But that situation could easily change. History shows us repeatedly that the Constitution is subject to human interpretation. Beliefs and values are bound to enter into those decisions. Where America stands on racism and discrimination today and tomorrow is where you stand, because the government is YOU.

CIVIL RIGHTS ORGANIZATIONS

Below is a list of civil rights organizations discussed in this book. There are of course other organizations dedicated to protecting the rights of many other racial, ethnic, and religious groups. Consult your local Yellow pages for organizations in your area. For nationwide organizations, see the *Encyclopedia of Associations* (Detroit: Gale Research), available at your local library.

American Civil Liberties Union (ACLU)
132 W. 43rd St.
New York, New York 10036

B'nai B'rith
1640 Rhode Island Ave. NW
Washington, DC 20036

Japanese American Citizens League
1730 Rhode Island Ave. NW #204
Washington, DC 20036

Martin Luther King Center
  for Nonviolent Social Change
449 Auburn Ave.
NE Atlanta, Georgia 30312

National Association for the
  Advancement of Colored People (NAACP)

4805 Mt. Hope Drive
Baltimore, Maryland 21215

People United to Save Humanity
(Operation PUSH)
930 E. 50th St.
Chicago, Illinois 60615

Urban League
500 E. 67th Street
New York, New York 10021

SOURCE NOTES

CHAPTER ONE

1. Gordon W. Allport, *The Nature of Prejudice*, x–xi.
2. Ibid., p. 6.
3. Lerone Bennett, Jr., *Before the Mayflower: A History of Black America*, p. 57.
4. Patricia and Fredrick McKissack, *The Civil Rights Movement in America from 1865 to Present*, p. 71.
5. *Time*, 2 February 1987, p. 21.
6. Patricia and Fredrick McKissack, *Jesse Jackson*, in press.

CHAPTER TWO

7. Gordon Allport, *The Nature of Prejudice*, p. 252.
8. Ibid., p. 255.
9. *St. Louis Business Journal*, Feb. 1989.
10. Op. Cit., Allport, p. 10.
11. Ibid., p. 92.
12. *Time*, 20 April 1987, p. 63.
13. Op. Cit., Allport, p. 15.
14. Thomas Kochman, *Black and White Styles in Conflict*, Chapter Three.
15. *St. Louis Post-Dispatch*, 7 March 1989.
16. Op. Cit., Allport, pp. 138–157.
17. *St. Louis American*, April 1985.
18. *St. Louis Post-Dispatch*, 8 April 1989.

CHAPTER THREE

19. Eugene Genovese, *Roll Jordan Roll: The World the Slaves Made,*
    p. 437.
20. Ibid., p. 441.
21. Ibid., p. 448.
22. *St. Louis Post-Dispatch,* 22 April 1989.

CHAPTER FOUR

23. Leslie Dunbar, *Minority Report: What Has Happened to Blacks,*
    Hispanics, American Indians and Other Minorities in the Eighties,
    pp. 156–171.
24. Patricia and Fredrick McKissack, *Civil Rights Movement in*
    America from 1865 to Present, pp. 10–25.
25. Ibid., pp. 40–55.
26. Ibid., p. 60.
27. Ibid., pp. 75–82.
28. Ibid., p. 82.
29. William Manchester, *The Glory and the Dream,* pp. 210–212.
30. Op. Cit., McKissack, *Civil Rights Movement,* pp. 150–156.
31. Op. Cit., Manchester, p. 235.
32. Stephen Oates, *Let the Trumpet Sound,* pp. 237–240.
33. Gerald Gill, *Meanness Mania: The Changed Mood,* pp. 60–73.
34. Op. Cit., Manchester, p. 239.

CHAPTER FIVE

35. Lerone Bennett, Jr., *Before the Mayflower: A History of Black*
    America, p. 258.
36. Patricia and Fredrick McKissack, *The Civil Rights Movement,*
    pp. 133–147.
37. Op. Cit., Bennett, pp. 337–338.
38. Ibid., p. 338.
39. Op. Cit., McKissack, p. 156.
40. Russell Adams, *Great American Negroes Past and Present,* "Marcus Garvey," p. 115.
41. Ibid., Various Selections.
42. Patricia McKissack, *Martin Luther King, Jr.: A Man to Remember,* pp. 49–51.
43. Stephen Oates, *Let the Trumpet Sound.*
44. Op. Cit., McKissack, *King,* Chapters 5 and 6.
45. Op. Cit., Adams, "Malcolm X," p. 31.

46. Op. Cit., McKissack, *Civil Rights,* p. 188.
47. McKissack, *Jesse Jackson,* in press.

CHAPTER SIX

48. Personal Interview with Portland Birch, May 1989.
49. Personal Interview with George Sakaguchi, April and May 1989.
50. JACL, *Redress: The American Promise,* p. 9.
51. JACL, *The Experience of Japanese Americans in the United States: A Teacher Resource Manual,* p. 31.
52. Richard and Maisie Conrat, *Redress: The American Promise,* pp. 15 and 17.
53. Ibid., p. 19.
54. Personal Interview with Beulah Mae Donald, May 1989.
55. *Ebony,* March 1988.

CHAPTER SEVEN

56. William Manchester, *The Glory and the Dream,* p. 410.
57. *Time,* 2 Feb. 1987, p. 21.
58. McKissack, *Civil Rights Movement,* "Whitney Young Cameo," p. 297.
59. Ibid., p. 271.
60. Ibid., pp. 265–270.
61. *Ebony,* June 1981, pp. 70–74.
62. *Ebony,* Dec. 1970, pp. 171–182.
63. Richard and Maisie Conrat, *Executive Order #9066,* pp. 26 and 33.
64. JACL, *Redress: The American Promise,* p. 19.
65. Eugene Genovese, *Roll Jordan Roll: The World the Slaves Made,* p. 366.
66. *St. Louis Post-Dispatch,* 5 June 1989.
67. Pontifical Commission, *The Church and Racism,* p. 34.

CHAPTER EIGHT

68. William Manchester, *The Glory and the Dream,* pp. 213–214.
69. Roger Hatch, *Beyond Opportunity—Jesse Jackson's Vision of America,* p. 87.
70. Public Service Ad, General Dynamics, as it appeared in *Time,* 2 Feb. 1987.

BIBLIOGRAPHY

BOOKS

Adams, Russell L. *Great Negroes Past and Present*. New York: Afro-Am Publishing Company, 1985.

Allport, Gordon W. *The Nature of Prejudice*. Garden City, N.Y.: Doubleday Anchor Books, 1958.

Bennett, Lerone, Jr. *Before the Mayflower—A History of Black America*. Chicago: Johnson Publishing Company, 1987.

Conrat, Richard and Maisie Conrat. *Executive Order 9066*. Los Angeles: California Historical Society, 1972.

Curtis, Michael. *The Great Political Theories*. New York: Avon Books, 1982.

Du Bois, W. E. B. *Against Racism*. Amherst: University of Massachusetts Press, 1985.

Dunbar, Leslie W. *Minority Report—What Has Happened to Blacks, Hispanics, American Indians and Other Minorities in the Eighties*. New York: Pantheon Books, 1984.

Genovese, Eugene D. *Roll, Jordan, Roll: The World the Slaves Made*. New York: Vintage Books, 1976.

Gill, Gerald. *Meanness Mania: The Changed Mood*. Washington, D.C.: Howard University Press, 1980.

Hatch, Roger D. *Beyond Opportunity*. Philadelphia: Fortress Press, 1988.

Klebanow, Diana, Franklin L. Jonas, and Ira M. Leonard. *Urban Legacy*. New York: New American Library, 1977.

Kochman, Thomas. *Black and White Styles in Conflict*. Chicago: University of Chicago Press, 1985.

Manchester, William. *The Glory and the Dream.* New York: Bantam Books, 1972.

McKissack, Patricia. *Martin Luther King: A Man to Remember.* Chicago: Children's Press, 1985.

McKissack, Patricia and Fredrick McKissack. *The Civil Rights Movement in America from 1865 to Present.* Chicago: Children's Press, 1987.

Oates, Stephen B. *Let the Trumpet Sound.* New York: Harper and Row, 1982.

Simmons, Gloria. *Black Culture.* New York: Holt Rinehart and Winston, 1972.

Sowell, Thomas. *The Economics and Politics of Race.* New York: William Morrow Company, 1983.

Tateishi, John. *And Justice for All: An Oral History of the Japanese American Detention Camps.* New York: Random House, 1984.

MAGAZINE ARTICLES

Fleishman, Alfred. "Ignorance Often Root of Race Problem." *St. Louis Business Journal,* February 6–12, 1989.

"Black vs. White in Howard Beach." *Time,* January 5, 1987.

"The Black Woman Who Beat the Ku Klux Klan." *Ebony,* March 1988.

"Finally I've Begun to Live Again." *Ebony,* December 1970.

"A Futile Veto on Civil Rights." *Time,* March 28, 1988.

"Interview with the Rev. Jesse Jackson." *Ebony,* June 1981.

REPORTS, PAPERS, AND PAMPHLETS

Brothers and Sisters to Us, U.S. Bishops' Pastoral Letter on Racism in Our Day. Produced by United States Catholic Conference, November 1979.

Redress: The American Promise. Produced by The Japanese American Citizens League, Legislative Education Committee, Washington, D.C.

The Experience of Japanese Americans in the United States: A Teacher Resource Manual. Prepared, printed, and distributed by an Advisory Council to the Ethnic Heritage Project of the Japanese American Citizens League; San Francisco: undated.

What We Have Seen and Heard: A Pastoral Letter on Evangelization from the Black Bishops of the United States. Cincinnati, Ohio: St. Anthony Messenger Press, 1984.

INDEX